PENGUIN BOOKS — GREAT IDEAS

The Lamp of Memory

John Ruskin
1819–1900

John Ruskin

The Lamp of Memory

PENGUIN BOOKS — GREAT IDEAS

PENGUIN BOOKS

Published by the Penguin Group
Penguin Books Ltd, 80 Strand, London wc2r orl, England
Penguin Group (USA) Inc., 375 Hudson Street, New York, New York 10014, USA
Penguin Group (Canada), 90 Eglinton Avenue East, Suite 700, Toronto, Ontario, Canada m4p 2y3
(a division of Pearson Penguin Canada Inc.)
Penguin Ireland, 25 St Stephen's Green, Dublin 2, Ireland
(a division of Penguin Books Ltd)
Penguin Group (Australia), 250 Camberwell Road, Camberwell, Victoria 3124, Australia
(a division of Pearson Australia Group Pty Ltd)
Penguin Books India Pvt Ltd, 11 Community Centre, Panchsheel Park, New Delhi – 110 017, India
Penguin Group (NZ), 67 Apollo Drive, Rosedale, North Shore 0632, New Zealand
(a division of Pearson New Zealand Ltd)
Penguin Books (South Africa) (Pty) Ltd, 24 Sturdee Avenue, Rosebank, Johannesburg 2196, South Africa

Penguin Books Ltd, Registered Offices: 80 Strand, London wc2r orl, England

www.penguin.com

'The Lamp of Memory' first published in *The Seven Lamps of Architecture*, 1849
'Cambridge School of Art: Inaugural Address' first published 1858
'Of Kings' Treasuries' first published in *Sesame and Lilies: Two Lectures*, 1865
'Traffic' first published in *The Crown of Wild Olive: Four Lectures on Industry and War* in 1866
This collection first published 2008
1

Set by Rowland Phototypesetting Ltd, Bury St Edmunds, Suffolk
Printed in England by Clays Ltd, St Ives plc

978-0-141-03667-0

www.greenpenguin.co.uk

Penguin Books is committed to a sustainable future
for our business, our readers and our planet.
The book in your hands is made from paper
certified by the Forest Stewardship Council.

Contents

The Lamp of Memory

Among the hours of his life to which the writer looks back with peculiar gratitude, as having been marked by more than ordinary fulness of joy or clearness of teaching, is one passed, now some years ago, near time of sunset, among the broken masses of pine forest which skirt the course of the Ain, above the village of Champagnole, in the Jura. It is a spot which has all the solemnity, with none of the savageness, of the Alps; where there is a sense of a great power beginning to be manifested in the earth, and of a deep and majestic concord in the rise of the long low lines of piny hills; the first utterance of those mighty mountain symphonies, soon to be more loudly lifted and wildly broken along the battlements of the Alps. But their strength is as yet restrained; and the far reaching ridges of pastoral mountain succeed each other, like the long and sighing swell which moves over quiet waters from some far off stormy sea. And there is a deep tenderness pervading that vast monotony. The destructive forces and the stern expression of the central ranges are alike withdrawn. No frost-ploughed, dust-encumbered paths of ancient glacier fret the soft Jura pastures; no splintered heaps of ruin break the fair ranks of her forest; no pale, defiled, or furious rivers send their rude and changeful ways among her rocks. Patiently, eddy by eddy, the clear green streams wind along their well-known beds; and under the dark quietness of the undisturbed pines, there spring up, year by year, such company of joyful flowers as I know not the like of among all the blessings of the earth. It was spring time, too; and all were coming forth in clusters crowded for very love; there was room enough for all, but they crushed their leaves into all manner of strange shapes only to be nearer each other. There was the wood anemone, star after star, closing every now and then into nebulae; and there was the oxalis, troop by troop, like virginal processions of the Mois de Marie, the dark vertical clefts in the limestone choked up with them as with heavy snow, and touched with ivy on the edges – ivy as light and lovely as the vine; and, ever and anon, a blue gush of violets, and cowslip bells in sunny places; and in the more open ground, the vetch, and comfrey, and mezereon, and the small sapphire buds of the Polygala Alpina, and the wild strawberry, just a blossom or two, all showered amidst the golden softness of deep, warm, amber-coloured moss. I came out presently on the edge of the ravine: the solemn murmur of its waters rose suddenly from beneath, mixed with the singing of the thrushes among the pine boughs; and, on the opposite side of the valley, walled all along as it was by grey cliffs of limestone, there was a hawk sailing slowly off their brow, touching them nearly with his wings, and with the shadows of the pines flickering upon his plumage from above; but with the fall of a hundred fathoms under his breast, and the curling pools of the green river gliding and glittering dizzily beneath him, their foam globes moving with him as he flew. It would be difficult to conceive a scene less dependent upon any other interest than that of its own secluded and serious beauty; but the writer well remembers the sudden blankness and chill which were cast upon it when he endeavoured, in order more strictly to arrive at the sources of its impressiveness, to imagine it, for a moment, a scene in some aboriginal forest of the New Continent. The flowers in an instant lost their light, the river its music; the hills became oppressively desolate; a heaviness in the boughs of the darkened forest showed how much of their former power had been dependent upon a life which was not theirs, how much of the glory of the imperishable, or continually renewed, creation is reflected from things more precious in their memories than it, in its renewing. Those ever springing flowers and ever flowing streams had been dyed by the deep colours of human endurance, valour, and virtue; and the crests of the sable hills that rose against the evening sky received a deeper worship, because their far shadows fell eastward over the iron walls of Joux, and the four-square keep of Granson.

It is as the centralization and protectress of this sacred influence, that Architecture is to be regarded by us with the most serious thought. We may live without her, and worship without her, but we cannot remember without her. How cold is all history, how lifeless all imagery, compared to that which the living nation writes, and the uncorrupted marble bears! – how many pages of doubtful record might we not often spare, for a few stones left one upon another! The ambition of the old Babel builders was well directed for this world: there are but two strong conquerors of the forgetfulness of men, Poetry and

Architecture; and the latter in some sort includes the former, and is mightier in its reality: it is well to have, not only what men have thought and felt, but what their hands have handled, and their strength wrought, and their eyes beheld, all the days of their life. The age of Homer is surrounded with darkness, his very personality with doubt. Not so that of Pericles: and the day is coming when we shall confess, that we have learned more of Greece out of the crumbled fragments of her sculpture than even from her sweet singers or soldier historians. And if indeed there be any profit in our knowledge of the past, or any joy in the thought of being remembered hereafter, which can give strength to present exertion, or patience to present endurance, there are two duties respecting national architecture whose importance it is impossible to overrate: the first, to render the architecture of the day, historical; and, the second, to preserve, as the most precious of inheritances, that of past ages.

It is in the first of these two directions that Memory may truly be said to be the Sixth Lamp of Architecture; for it is in becoming memorial or monumental that a true perfection is attained by civil and domestic buildings; and this partly as they are, with such a view, built in a more stable manner, and partly as their decorations are consequently animated by a metaphorical or historical meaning.

As regards domestic buildings, there must always be a certain limitation to views of this kind in the power, as well as in the hearts, of men; still I cannot but think it an evil sign of a people when their houses are built to last for one generation only. There is a sanctity in a good man's house which cannot be renewed in every tenement that rises on its ruins: and I believe that good men would generally feel this; and that having spent their lives happily and honourably, they would be grieved, at the close of them, to think that the place of their earthly abode, which had seen, and seemed almost to sympathize in, all their honour, their gladness, or their suffering, – that this, with all the record it bare of them, and of all material things that they had loved and ruled over, and set the stamp of themselves upon – was to be swept away, as soon as there was room made for them in the grave; that no respect was to be shown to it, no affection felt for it, no good to be drawn from it by their children; that though there was a monument in the church, there was no warm monument in the hearth and house to them; that all that they ever treasured was despised, and the places that had sheltered and comforted them were dragged down to the dust. I say that a good man would fear this; and that, far more, a good son, a noble descendant, would fear doing it to his father's house. I say that if men lived like men indeed, their houses would be temples – temples which we should hardly dare to injure, and in which it would make us holy to be permitted to live; and there must be a strange dissolution of natural affection, a strange unthankfulness for all that homes have given and parents taught, a strange consciousness that we have been unfaithful to our fathers' honour, or that our own lives are not such as would make our dwellings sacred to our children, when each man would fain build to himself, and build for the little revolution of his own life only. And I look upon those pitiful concretions of lime and clay which spring up, in mildewed forwardness, out of the kneaded fields about our capital – upon those thin, tottering, foundationless shells of splintered wood and imitated stone – upon those gloomy rows of formal-ized minuteness, alike without difference and without fellowship, as solitary as similar – not merely with the careless disgust of an offended eye, not merely with sorrow for a desecrated landscape, but with a painful foreboding that the roots of our national greatness must be deeply cankered when they are thus loosely struck in their native ground; that those comfortless and unhonoured dwellings are the signs of a great and spread-ing spirit of popular discontent; that they mark the time when every man's aim is to be in some more elevated sphere than his natural one, and every man's past life is his habitual scorn; when men build in the hope of leaving the places they have built, and live in the hope of forget-ting the years that they have lived; when the comfort, the peace, the religion of home have ceased to be felt; and the crowded tenements of a struggling and restless population differ only from the tents of the Arab or the Gipsy by their less healthy openness to the air of heaven, and less happy choice of their spot of earth; by their sacrifice of liberty without the gain of rest, and of stability without the luxury of change.

This is no slight, no consequenceless evil; it is omin-ous, infectious, and fecund of other fault and misfortune. When men do not love their hearths, nor reverence their thresholds, it is a sign that they have dishonoured both, and that they have never acknowledged the true univer-sality of that Christian worship which was indeed to

supersede the idolatry, but not the piety, of the pagan.
Our God is a household God, as well as a heavenly one;
He has an altar in every man's dwelling; let men look to
it when they rend it lightly and pour out its ashes. It is
not a question of mere ocular delight, it is no question
of intellectual pride, or of cultivated and critical fancy,
how, and with what aspect of durability and of complete-
ness, the domestic buildings of a nation shall be raised.
It is one of those moral duties, not with more impunity
to be neglected because the perception of them depends
on a finely toned and balanced conscientiousness, to
build our dwellings with care, and patience, and fondness, and diligent completion, and with a view to their
duration at least for such a period as, in the ordinary
course of national revolutions, might be supposed likely
to extend to the entire alteration of the direction of local
interests. This at the least; but it would be better if, in
every possible instance, men built their own houses on
a scale commensurate rather with their condition at the
commencement, than their attainments at the termina-
tion, of their worldly career; and built them to stand as
long as human work at its strongest can be hoped to
stand; recording to their children what they had been,
and from what, if so it had been permitted them, they
had risen. And when houses are thus built, we may
have that true domestic architecture, the beginning of
all other, which does not disdain to treat with respect
and thoughtfulness the small habitation as well as the
large, and which invests with the dignity of contented
manhood the narrowness of worldly circumstance.

I look to this spirit of honourable, proud, peaceful

7

self-possession, this abiding wisdom of contented life, as probably one of the chief sources of great intellectual power in all ages, and beyond dispute as the very primal source of the great architecture of old Italy and France. To this day, the interest of their fairest cities depends, not on the isolated richness of palaces, but on the cherished and exquisite decoration of even the smallest tenements of their proud periods. The most elaborate piece of architecture in Venice is a small house at the head of the Grand Canal, consisting of a ground floor with two storeys above, three windows in the first, and two in the second. Many of the most exquisite buildings are on the narrower canals, and of no larger dimensions. One of the most interesting pieces of fifteenth-century architecture in North Italy, is a small house in a back street, behind the market-place of Vicenza; it bears date 1481, and the motto, *Il. n'est. rose. sans. épine.*; it has also only a ground floor and two storeys, with three windows in each, separated by rich flower-work, and with balconies, supported, the central one by an eagle with open wings, the lateral ones by winged griffins standing on cornucopiae. The idea that a house must be large in order to be well built, is altogether of modern growth, and is parallel with the idea, that no picture can be historical, except of a size admitting figures larger than life.

I would have, then, our ordinary dwelling-houses built to last, and built to be lovely; as rich and full of pleasantness as may be, within and without; with what degree of likeness to each other in style and manner, I will say presently, under another head; but, at all events, with such differences as might suit and express each man's character and occupation, and partly his history. This right over the house, I conceive, belongs to its first builder, and is to be respected by his children; and it would be well that blank stones should be left in places, to be inscribed with a summary of his life and of its experience, raising thus the habitation into a kind of monument, and developing, into more systematic instructiveness, that good custom which was of old universal, and which still remains among some of the Swiss and Germans, of acknowledging the grace of God's permission to build and possess a quiet resting-place, in such sweet words as may well close our speaking of these things. I have taken them from the front of a cottage lately built among the green pastures which descend from the village of Grindelwald to the lower glacier: –

> 'Mit herzlichem Vertrauen
> Hat Johannes Mooter und Maria Rubi
> Dieses Haus bauen lassen.
> Der liebe Gott woll uns bewahren
> Vor allem Unglück und Gefahren,
> Und es in Segen lassen stehn
> Auf der Reise durch diese Jammerzeit
> Nach dem himmlischen Paradiese,
> Wo alle Frommen wohnen,
> Da wird Gott sie belohnen
> Mit der Friedenskrone
>   Zu alle Ewigkeit.'*

* *Mit herzlichem Vertrauen . . . alle Ewigkeit*: 'With heartfelt trust | Have Johannes Mooter and Maria Rubi | Had this house built. | The dear God will shield us | From all misfortune and danger | And let

In public buildings the historical purpose should be still more definite. It is one of the advantages of Gothic architecture, – I use the word Gothic in the most extended sense as broadly opposed to classical, – that it admits of a richness of record altogether unlimited. Its minute and multitudinous sculptural decorations afford means of expressing, either symbolically or literally, all that need be known of national feeling or achievement. More decoration will, indeed, be usually required than can take so elevated a character; and much, even in the most thoughtful periods, has been left to the freedom of fancy, or suffered to consist of mere repetitions of some national bearing or symbol. It is, however, generally unwise, even in mere surface ornament, to surrender the power and privilege of variety which the spirit of Gothic architecture admits; much more in important features – capitals of columns or bosses, and string-courses, as of course in all confessed bas-reliefs. Better the rudest work that tells a story or records a fact, than the richest without meaning. There should not be a single ornament put upon great civic buildings, without some intellectual intention. Actual representation of history has in modern times been checked by a difficulty, mean indeed, but steadfast; that of unmanageable costume: nevertheless, by a sufficiently bold imaginative treatment, and frank use of symbols, all such obstacles may be vanquished; not perhaps in the degree necessary

---

it stand in blessedness | On this journey, through this time of sorrow | To the heavenly Paradise | Where all good people dwell, | There will God reward them | With the Crown of Peace | To all eternity.'

to produce sculpture in itself satisfactory, but at all events so as to enable it to become a grand and expressive element of architectural composition. Take, for example, the management of the capitals of the ducal palace at Venice. History, as such, was indeed entrusted to the painters of its interior, but every capital of its arcades was filled with meaning. The large one, the corner stone of the whole, next the entrance, was devoted to the symbolization of Abstract Justice; above it is a sculpture of the Judgment of Solomon, remarkable for a beautiful subjection in its treatment to its decorative purpose. The figures, if the subject had been entirely composed of them, would have awkwardly interrupted the line of the angle, and diminished its apparent strength; and therefore in the midst of them, entirely without relation to them, and indeed actually between the executioner and interceding mother, there rises the ribbed trunk of a massy tree, which supports and continues the shaft of the angle, and whose leaves above overshadow and enrich the whole. The capital below bears among its leafage a throned figure of Justice, Trajan doing justice to the widow, Aristotle 'che die legge,' and one or two other subjects now unintelligible from decay. The capitals next in order represent the virtues and vices in succession, as preservative or destructive of national peace and power, concluding with Faith, with the inscription 'Fides optima in Deo est.' A figure is seen on the opposite side of the capital, worshipping the sun. After these, one or two capitals are fancifully decorated with birds, and then come a series representing, first the various fruits, then the national costumes, and then the animals of the various countries subject to Venetian rule.

Now, not to speak of any more important public building, let us imagine our own India House adorned in this way, by historical or symbolical sculpture: massively built in the first place; then chased with bas-reliefs of our Indian battles, and fretted with carvings of Oriental foliage, or inlaid with Oriental stones; and the more important members of its decoration composed of groups of Indian life and landscape, and prominently expressing the phantasms of Hindoo worship in their subjection to the Cross. Would not one such work be better than a thousand histories? If, however, we have not the invention necessary for such efforts, or if, which is probably one of the most noble excuses we can offer for our deficiency in such matters, we have less pleasure in talking about ourselves, even in marble, than the Continental nations, at least we have no excuse for any want of care in the points which insure the building's endurance. And as this question is one of great interest in its relations to the choice of various modes of decoration, it will be necessary to enter into it at some length.

The benevolent regards and purposes of men in masses seldom can be supposed to extend beyond their own generation. They may look to posterity as an audience, may hope for its attention, and labour for its praise: they may trust to its recognition of unacknowledged merit, and demand its justice for contemporary wrong. But all this is mere selfishness, and does not involve the slightest regard to, or consideration of, the interest of those by whose numbers we would fain swell the circle of our flatterers, and by whose authority we would gladly support our presently disputed claims. The idea of self-denial for the sake of posterity, of practising present economy for the sake of debtors yet unborn, of planting forests that our descendants may live under their shade, or of raising cities for future nations to inhabit, never, I suppose, efficiently takes place among publicly recognized motives of exertion. Yet these are not the less our duties; nor is our part fitly sustained upon the earth, unless the range of our intended and deliberate usefulness include, not only the companions but the successors of our pilgrimage. God has lent us the earth for our life; it is a great entail. It belongs as much to those who are to come after us, and whose names are already written in the book of creation, as to us; and we have no right, by anything that we do or neglect, to involve them in unnecessary penalties, or deprive them of benefits which it was in our power to bequeath. And this the more, because it is one of the appointed conditions of the labour of men that, in proportion to the time between the seed-sowing and the harvest, is the fulness of the fruit; and that generally, therefore, the farther off we place our aim, and the less we desire to be ourselves the witnesses of what we have laboured for, the more wide and rich will be the measure of our success. Men cannot benefit those that are with them as they can benefit those who come after them; and of all the pulpits from which human voice is ever sent forth, there is none from which it reaches so far as from the grave.

Nor is there, indeed, any present loss, in such respect, for futurity. Every human action gains in honour, in grace, in all true magnificence, by its regard to things that are to come. It is the far sight, the quiet and confident patience, that, above all other attributes, separate man from man, and near him to his Maker; and there is no action nor art, whose majesty we may not measure by this test. Therefore, when we build, let us think that we build for ever. Let it not be for present delight, nor for present use alone; let it be such work as our descendants will thank us for, and let us think, as we lay stone on stone, that a time is to come when those stones will be held sacred because our hands have touched them, and that men will say as they look upon the labour and wrought substance of them, 'See! this our fathers did for us.' For, indeed, the greatest glory of a building is not in its stones, nor in its gold. Its glory is in its Age, and in that deep sense of voicefulness, of stern watching, of mysterious sympathy, nay, even of approval or condemnation, which we feel in walls that have long been washed by the passing waves of humanity. It is in their lasting witness against men, in their quiet contrast with the transitional character of all things, in the strength which, through the lapse of seasons and times, and the decline and birth of dynasties, and the changing of the face of the earth, and of the limits of the sea, maintains its sculptured shapeliness for a time insuperable, connects forgotten and following ages with each other, and half constitutes the identity, as it concentrates the sympathy, of nations: it is in that golden stain of time, that we are to look for the real light, and colour, and preciousness of architecture; and it is not until a building has assumed this character, till it has been entrusted with the fame, and hallowed by the deeds of men, till its walls have been witnesses of suffering, and its pillars rise out of the shadows of death, that its existence, more lasting as it is than that of the natural objects of the world around it, can be gifted with even so much as these possess, of language and of life . . .

Do not let us talk then of restoration. The thing is a Lie from beginning to end. You may make a model of a building as you may of a corpse, and your model may have the shell of the old walls within it as your cast might have the skeleton, with what advantage I neither see nor care: but the old building is destroyed, and that more totally and mercilessly than if it had sunk into a heap of dust, or melted into a mass of clay: more has been gleaned out of desolated Nineveh than ever will be out of rebuilt Milan. But, it is said, there may come a necessity for restoration! Granted. Look the necessity full in the face, and understand it on its own terms. It is a necessity for destruction. Accept it as such, pull the building down, throw its stones into neglected corners, make ballast of them, or mortar, if you will; but do it honestly, and do not set up a Lie in their place. And look that necessity in the face before it comes, and you may prevent it. The principle of modern times, (a principle which, I believe, at least in France, to be *systematically acted on by the masons*, in order to find themselves work, as the abbey of St Ouen was pulled down by the magistrates of the town by way of giving work to some vagrants,) is to neglect buildings first, and restore them afterwards. Take proper care of your monuments, and you will not need to restore them. A few sheets of lead put in time upon a roof, a few dead leaves and sticks swept in time out of a water-course, will save both roof and walls from ruin. Watch an old building with an anxious care; guard it as best you may, and at *any* cost, from every influence of dilapidation. Count its stones as you would jewels of a crown; set watches about it as if at the gates of a besieged city; bind it together with iron where it loosens; stay it with timber where it declines; do not care about the unsightliness of the aid: better a crutch than a lost limb; and do this tenderly, and reverently, and continually, and many a generation will still be born and pass away beneath its shadow. Its evil day must come at last; but let it come declaredly and openly, and let no dishonouring and false substitute deprive it of the funeral offices of memory.

Of more wanton or ignorant ravage it is vain to speak; my words will not reach those who commit them,[1] and yet, be it heard or not, I must not leave the truth unstated, that it is again no question of expediency or feeling whether we shall preserve the buildings of past times or not. *We have no right whatever to touch them.* They are not ours. They belong partly to those who built them, and partly to all the generations of mankind who are to follow us. The dead have still their right in them: that which they laboured for, the praise of achievement or the expression of religious feeling, or whatsoever else it might be which in those buildings they intended to be permanent, we have no right to obliterate. What we have ourselves built, we are at liberty to throw down; but what other men gave their strength and wealth and life to accomplish, their right over does not pass away with their death; still less is the right to the use of what they have left vested in us only. It belongs to all their successors. It may hereafter be a subject of sorrow, or a cause of injury, to millions, that we have consulted our present convenience by casting down such buildings as we choose to dispense with. That sorrow, that loss, we have no right to inflict. Did the cathedral of Avranches belong to the mob who destroyed it, any more than it did to us, who walk in sorrow to and fro over its foundation? Neither does any building whatever belong to those mobs who do violence to it. For a mob it is, and must be always; it matters not whether enraged, or in deliberate folly; whether countless, or sitting in committees; the people who destroy anything causelessly are a mob, and Architecture is always destroyed causelessly. A fair building is necessarily worth the ground it stands upon, and will be so until Central Africa and America shall have become as populous as Middlesex: nor is any cause whatever valid as a ground for its destruction. If ever valid, certainly not now, when the place both of the past and future is too much usurped in our minds by the restless and discontented present. The very quietness of nature is gradually withdrawn from us; thousands who once in their necessarily prolonged travel were subjected to an influence, from the silent sky and slumbering fields, more effectual than known or confessed, now bear with them even there the ceaseless fever of their life; and along the iron veins that traverse the frame of our country, beat and flow the fiery pulses of its exertion, hotter and faster every hour. All vitality is concentrated through those throbbing arteries into the central cities; the country is passed over like a green sea by narrow bridges, and we are thrown back in continually closer crowds upon the city gates. The only influence which can in any wise *there* take the place of that of the woods and fields, is the power of ancient Architecture. Do not part with it for the sake of the formal square, or of the fenced and planted walk, nor of the goodly street nor opened quay. The pride of a city is not in these. Leave them to the crowd; but remember that there will surely be some within the circuit of the disquieted walls who would ask for some other spots than these wherein to walk; for some other forms to meet their sight familiarly: like him who sat so often where the sun struck from the west, to watch the lines of the dome of Florence drawn on the deep sky, or like those, his Hosts, who could bear daily to behold, from their palace chambers, the places where their fathers lay at rest, at the meeting of the dark streets of Verona.

Notes

1. No, indeed! – any more wasted words than mine through-out life, or bread cast on more bitter waters, I never heard of. This closing paragraph of the sixth chapter is the best, I think, in the book, – and the vainest. [1880.]

Cambridge School of Art: Inaugural Address (1858)

I suppose the persons interested in establishing a School of Art for workmen may in the main be divided into two classes, namely, first, those who chiefly desire to make the men themselves happier, wiser, and better; and secondly, those who desire to enable them to produce better and more valuable work. These two objects may, of course, be kept both in view at the same time; nevertheless, there is a wide difference in the spirit with which we shall approach our task, according to the motive of these two which weighs most with us – a difference great enough to divide, as I have said, the promoters of any such scheme into two distinct classes; one philanthropic in the gist of its aim, and the other commercial in the gist of its aim; one desiring the workman to be better informed chiefly for his own sake, and the other chiefly that he may be enabled to produce for us commodities precious in themselves, and which shall successfully compete with those of other countries.

And this separation in motives must lead also to a distinction in the machinery of the work. The philanthropists address themselves, not to the artisan merely, but to the labourer in general, desiring in any possible way to refine the habits or increase the happiness of our whole working population, by giving them new recreations or new thoughts: and the principles of

Art-education adopted in a school which has this wide but somewhat indeterminate aim, are, or should be, very different from those adopted in a school meant for the special instruction of the artisan in his own business. I do not think this distinction is yet firmly enough fixed in our minds, or calculated upon in our plans of operation. We have hitherto acted, it seems to me, under a vague impression that the arts of drawing and painting might be, up to a certain point, taught in a general way to every one, and would do every one equal good; and that each class of operatives might afterwards bring this general knowledge into use in their own trade, according to its requirements. Now, that is not so. A wood-carver needs for his business to learn drawing in quite a different way from a china-painter, and a jeweller from a worker in iron. They must be led to study quite different characters in the natural forms they introduce in their various manufacture. It is no use to teach an iron-worker to observe the down on a peach, and of none to teach laws of atmospheric effect to a carver in wood. So far as their business is concerned, their brains would be vainly occupied by such things, and they would be prevented from pursuing, with enough distinctness or intensity, the qualities of Art which can alone be expressed in the materials with which they each have to do.

Now, I believe it to be wholly impossible to teach special application of Art principles to various trades in a single school. That special application can be only learned rightly by the experience of years in the particular work required. The power of each material, and the difficulties connected with its treatment, are not so much to be taught as to be felt; it is only by repeated touch and continued trial beside the forge or the furnace, that the goldsmith can find out how to govern his gold, or the glass-worker his crystal; and it is only by watching and assisting the actual practice of a master in the business, that the apprentice can learn the efficient secrets of manipulation, or perceive the true limits of the involved conditions of design. It seems to me, therefore, that all idea of reference to definite businesses should be abandoned in such schools as that just established: we can have neither the materials, the conveniences, nor the empirical skill in the master, necessary to make such teaching useful. All specific Art-teaching must be given in schools established by each trade for itself: and when our operatives are a little more enlightened on these matters, there will be found, as I have already stated in my lectures on the political economy of Art, absolute necessity for the establishment of guilds of trades in an active and practical form, for the purposes of ascertaining the principles of Art proper to their business, and instructing their apprentices in them, as well as making experiments on materials, and on newly invented methods of procedure; besides many other functions which I cannot now enter into account of. All this for the present, and in a school such as this, I repeat, we cannot hope for: we shall obtain no satisfactory result, unless we give up such hope, and set ourselves to teaching the operative, however employed – be he farmer's labourer, or manufacturer's; be he mechanic, artificer, shopman, sailor, or ploughman – teaching, I say, as far as we can, one and the same thing to all; namely, Sight.

Not a slight thing to teach, this: perhaps, on the whole, the most important thing to be taught in the whole range of teaching. To be taught to read – what is the use of that, if you know not whether what you read is false or true? To be taught to write or to speak – but what is the use of speaking, if you have nothing to say? To be taught to think – nay, what is the use of being able to think, if you have nothing to think of? But to be taught to see is to gain word and thought at once, and both true. There is a vague acknowledgment of this in the way people are continually expressing their longing for light, until all the common language of our prayers and hymns has sunk into little more than one monotonous metaphor, dimly twisted into alternate languages, – asking first in Latin to be illuminated; and then in English to be enlightened; and then in Latin again to be delivered out of obscurity; and then in English to be delivered out of darkness; and then for beams, and rays, and suns, and stars, and lamps, until sometimes one wishes that, at least for religious purposes, there were no such words as light or darkness in existence. Still, the main instinct which makes people endure this perpetuity of repetition is a true one; only the main thing they want and ought to ask for is, not light, but Sight. It doesn't matter how much light you have if you don't know how to use it. It may very possibly put out your eyes, instead of helping them. Besides, we want, in this world of ours, very often to be able to see in the dark – that's the great gift of all; – but at any rate to see no matter by what light, so only we can see things as they are. On my word, we should soon make it a different world, if we could get but a little

– ever so little – of the dervish's ointment in the *Arabian Nights*, not to show us the treasures of the earth, but the facts of it.

However, whether these things be generally true or not, at all events it is certain that our immediate business, in such a school as this, will prosper more by attending to eyes than to hands; we shall always do most good by simply endeavouring to enable the student to see natural objects clearly and truly. We ought not even to try too strenuously to give him the power of representing them. That power may be acquired, more or less, by exercises which are no wise conducive to accuracy of sight: and, *vice versâ*, accuracy of sight may be gained by exercises which in no wise conduce to ease of representation. For instance, it very much assists the power of drawing to spend many hours in the practice of washing in flat tints; but all this manual practice does not in the least increase the student's power of determining what the tint of a given object actually is. He would be more advanced in the knowledge of the facts by a single hour of well-directed and well-*corrected* effort, rubbing out and putting in again, lightening, and darkening, and scratching, and blotching, in patient endeavours to obtain concordance with fact, issuing perhaps, after all, in total destruction or unpresentability of the drawing; but also in acute perception of the things he has been attempting to copy in it. Of course, there is always a vast temptation, felt both by the master and student, to struggle towards visible results, and obtain something beautiful, creditable, or saleable, in way of actual drawing: but the more I see of schools, the more reason I see to look with doubt upon those which produce too many showy and complete works by pupils. A showy work will always be found, on stern examination of it, to have been done by some conventional rule; – some servile compliance with directions which the student does not see the reason for; and representation of truths which he has not himself perceived: the execution of such drawings will be found monotonous and lifeless; their light and shade specious and formal, but false. A drawing which the pupil has learned much in doing, is nearly always full of blunders and mishaps, and it is highly necessary for the formation of a truly public or universal school of Art, that the masters should not try to conceal or anticipate such blunders, but only seek to employ, the pupil's time so as to get the most precious results for his understanding and his heart, not for his hand.

For, observe, the best that you can do in the production of drawing, or of draughtsmanship, must always be nothing in itself, unless the whole life be given to it. An amateur's drawing, or a workman's drawing – anybody's drawing but an artist's, is always valueless in itself. It may be . . . most precious as a memorial, or as a gift, or as a means of noting useful facts; but as *Art*, an amateur's drawing is always wholly worthless; and it ought to be one of our great objects to make the pupil understand and feel that, and prevent his trying to make his valueless work look, in some superficial, hypocritical, eye-catching, penny-catching way, like work that is really good.

If, therefore, we have to do with pupils belonging to the higher ranks of life, our main duty will be to make them good judges of Art, rather than artists; for though I had a month to speak to you, instead of an hour, time would fail me if I tried to trace the various ways in which we suffer, nationally, for want of powers of enlightened judgment of Art in our upper and middle classes. Not that this judgment can ever be obtained without discipline of the hand: no man ever was a thorough judge of painting who could not draw; but the drawing should only be thought of as a means of fixing his attention upon the subtleties of the Art put before him, or of enabling him to record such natural facts as are necessary for comparison with it. I should also attach the greatest importance to severe limitation of choice in the examples submitted to him. To study one good master till you understand him will teach you more than a superficial acquaintance with a thousand: power of criticism does not consist in knowing the names or the manner of many painters, but in discerning the excellence of a few.

If, on the contrary, our teaching is addressed more definitely to the operative, we need not endeavour to render his powers of criticism very acute. About many forms of existing Art, the less he knows the better. His sensibilities are to be cultivated with respect to nature chiefly; and his imagination, if possible, to be developed, even though somewhat to the disadvantage of his judgment. It is better that his work should be bold, than faultless: and better that it should be delightful, than discreet.

And this leads me to the second, or commercial, question; namely, how to get from the workman, after we have trained him, the best and most precious work, so as to enable ourselves to compete with foreign countries, or develop new branches of commerce in our own.

Many of us, perhaps, are under the impression that plenty of schooling will do this; that plenty of lecturing will do it; that sending abroad for patterns will do it; or that patience, time, and money, and goodwill may do it. And, alas, none of these things, nor all of them put together, will do it. If you want really good work, such as will be acknowledged by all the world, there is but one way of getting it, and that is a difficult one. You may offer any premium you choose for it – but you will find it can't be done for premiums. You may send for patterns to the antipodes – but you will find it can't be done upon patterns. You may lecture on the principles of Art to every school in the kingdom – and you will find it can't be done upon principles. You may wait patiently for the progress of the age – and you will find your Art is unprogressive. Or you may set yourselves impatiently to urge it by the inventions of the age – and you will find your chariot of Art entirely immovable either by screw or paddle. There's no way of getting good Art, I repeat, but one – at once the simplest and most difficult – namely, to enjoy it. Examine the history of nations, and you will find this great fact clear and unmistakable on the front of it – that good Art has only been produced by nations who rejoiced in it; fed themselves with it, as if it were bread; basked in it, as if it were sunshine; shouted at the sight of it; danced with the delight of it; quarrelled for it; fought for it; starved for it; did, in fact, precisely the opposite with it of what we want to do with it – they made it to keep, and we to sell.

And truly this is a serious difficulty for us as a commercial nation. The very primary motive with which we set about the business, makes the business impossible. The first and absolute condition of the thing's ever becoming saleable is, that we shall make it without wanting to sell it; nay, rather with a determination not to sell it at any price, if once we get hold of it. Try to make your Art popular, cheap – a fair article for your foreign market; and the foreign market will always show something better. But make it only to please yourselves, and even be resolved that you won't let anybody else have any; and forthwith you will find everybody else wants it. And observe, the insuperable difficulty is this making it to please ourselves, while we are incapable of pleasure. Take, for instance, the simplest example, which we can all understand, in the art of dress. We have made a great fuss about the patterns of silk lately; wanting to vie with Lyons, and make a Paris of London. Well, we may try for ever: so long as we don't really enjoy silk patterns, we shall never get any. And we don't enjoy them. Of course, all ladies like their dresses to sit well, and be becoming; but of real enjoyment of the beauty of the silk, for the silk's own sake, I find none; for the test of that enjoyment is, that they would like it also to sit well, and look well, on somebody else. The pleasure of being well dressed, or even of seeing well-dressed people – for I will suppose in my fair hearers that degree of unselfishness – be that pleasure great or small, is quite a different thing from delight in the beauty and play of the silken folds and colours themselves, for their own gorgeousness or grace.

I have just had a remarkable proof of the total want of this feeling in the modern mind. I was staying part of this summer in Turin, for the purpose of studying one of the Paul Veroneses there – the presentation of the Queen of Sheba to Solomon. Well, one of the most notable characters in this picture is the splendour of its silken dresses: and, in particular, there was a piece of white brocade, with designs upon it in gold, which it was one of my chief objects in stopping at Turin to copy. You may, perhaps, be surprised at this; but I must just note in passing, that I share this weakness of enjoying dress patterns with all good students and all good painters. It doesn't matter what school they belong to, – Fra Angelico, Perugino, John Bellini, Giorgione, Titian, Tintoret, Veronese, Leonardo da Vinci – no matter how they differ in other respects, all of them like dress patterns; and what is more, the nobler the painter is, the surer he is to do his patterns well.

I stayed then, as I say, to make a study of this white brocade. It generally happens in public galleries that the best pictures are the worst placed; and this Veronese is not only hung at considerable height above the eye, but over a door, through which, however, as all the visitors to the gallery must pass, they cannot easily overlook the picture, though they would find great difficulty in examining it. Beside this door, I had a stage erected for my work, which being of some height and rather in a corner, enabled me to observe, without being observed myself, the impression made by the picture on the various visitors. It seemed to me that if ever a work of Art caught popular attention, this ought to do so. It was of very large size; of brilliant colour, and of agreeable subject. There are about twenty figures in it, the principal ones being life size: that of Solomon, though in the shade, is by far the most perfect conception of the young king in his pride of wisdom and beauty which I know in the range of Italian art; the queen is one of the loveliest of Veronese's female figures; all the accessories are full of grace and imagination; and the finish of the whole so perfect that one day I was upwards of two hours vainly trying to render, with perfect accuracy, the curves of two leaves of the brocaded silk. The English travellers used to walk through the room in considerable numbers; and were invariably directed to the picture by their laquais de place, if they missed seeing it themselves. And to this painting – in which it took me six weeks to examine rightly two figures – I found that on an average, the English traveller who was doing Italy conscientiously, and seeing everything as he thought he ought, gave about half or three-quarters of a minute; but the flying or fashionable traveller, who came to do as much as he could in a given time, never gave more than a single glance, most of such people turning aside instantly to a bad landscape hung on the right, containing a vigorously painted white wall, and an opaque green moat. What especially impressed me, however, was that none of the ladies ever stopped to look at the dresses in the Veronese. Certainly they were far more beautiful than any in the shops in the great square, yet no one ever noticed them. Sometimes when any nice, sharp-looking, bright-eyed girl came into the room, I used to watch her all the way, thinking – 'Come, at least *you'll* see what the

Queen of Sheba has got on.' But no – on she would come carelessly, with a little toss of the head, apparently signifying, 'nothing in *this* room worth looking at – except myself,' and so trip through the door, and away.

The fact is, we don't care for pictures: in very deed we don't. The Academy exhibition is a thing to talk of and to amuse vacant hours; those who are rich amongst us buy a painting or two, for mixed reasons, sometimes to fill the corner of a passage – sometimes to help the drawing-room talk before dinner – sometimes because the painter is fashionable – occasionally because he is poor – not unfrequently that we may have a collection of specimens of painting, as we have specimens of minerals or butterflies – and in the best and rarest case of all, because we have really, as we call it, taken a fancy to the picture; meaning the same sort of fancy which one would take to a pretty arm-chair or a newly-shaped decanter. But as for real love of the picture, and joy of it when we have got it, I do not believe it is felt by one in a thousand.

I am afraid this apathy of ours will not be easily conquered; but even supposing it should, and that we should begin to enjoy pictures properly, and that the supply of good ones increased as in that case it *would* increase – then comes another question. Perhaps some of my hearers this evening may occasionally have heard it stated of me that I am rather apt to contradict myself. I hope I am exceedingly apt to do so. I never met with a question yet, of any importance, which did not need, for the right solution of it, at least one positive and one negative answer, like an equation of the second degree. Mostly, matters of any consequence are three-sided, or four-sided, or polygonal; and the trotting round a poly-gon is severe work for people any way stiff in their opinions. For myself, I am never satisfied that I have handled a subject properly till I have contradicted myself at least three times: but once must do for this evening. I have just said that there is no chance of our getting good Art unless we delight in it: next I say, and just as positively, that there is no chance of our getting good Art unless we resist our delight in it. We must love it first, and restrain our love for it afterwards.

This sounds strange; and yet I assure you it is true. In fact, whenever anything does not sound strange, you may generally doubt its being true; for all truth is wonderful. But take an instance in physical matters, of the same kind of contradiction. Suppose you were explaining to a young student in astronomy how the earth was kept steady in its orbit; you would have to state to him – would you not? – that the earth always had a tendency to fall to the sun; and that also it always had a tendency to fly away from the sun. These are two precisely contrary statements for him to digest at his leisure, before he can understand how the earth moves. Now, in like manner, when Art is set in its true and serviceable course, it moves under the luminous attrac-tion of pleasure on the one side, and with a stout moral purpose of going about some useful business on the other. If the artist works without delight, he passes away into space, and perishes of cold: if he works only for delight, he falls into the sun, and extinguishes himself in ashes. On the whole, this last is the fate, I do not say the most to be feared, but which Art has generally hitherto suffered, and which the great nations of the earth have suffered with it.

For, while most distinctly you may perceive in past history that Art has never been produced, except by nations who took pleasure in it, just as assuredly, and even more plainly, you may perceive that Art has always destroyed the power and life of those who pursued it for pleasure only. Surely this fact must have struck you as you glanced at the career of the great nations of the earth: surely it must have occurred to you as a point for serious questioning, how far, even in our days, we were wise in promoting the advancement of pleasures which appeared as yet only to have corrupted the souls and numbed the strength of those who attained to them. I have been complaining of England that she despises the Arts; but I might, with still more appearance of justice, complain that she does not rather dread them than despise. For, what has been the source of the ruin of nations since the world began? Has it been plague, or famine, earthquake-shock or volcano-flame? None of these ever prevailed against a great people, so as to make their name pass from the earth. In every period and place of national decline, you will find other causes than these at work to bring it about, namely, luxury, effeminacy, love of pleasure, fineness in Art, ingenuity in enjoyment. What is the main lesson which, as far as we seek any in our classical reading, we gather for our youth from ancient history? Surely this – that simplicity of life, of language, and of manners gives strength to a nation; and that luxuriousness of life, subtlety of language, and smoothness of manners bring weakness and destruction on a nation. While men possess little and desire less, they remain brave and noble: while they are scornful of all the arts of luxury, and are in the sight of other nations as barbarians, their swords are irresistible and their sway illimitable: but let them become sensitive to the refinements of taste, and quick in the capacities of pleasure, and, that instant, the fingers, that had grasped the iron rod, fail from the golden sceptre. You cannot charge me with any exaggeration in this matter; it is impossible to state the truth too strongly, or as too universal. For ever you will see the rude and simple nation at once more virtuous and more victorious than one practised in the arts. Watch how the Lydian is overthrown by the Persian; the Persian by the Athenian; the Athenian by the Spartan; then the whole of polished Greece by the rougher Roman; the Roman, in his turn refined, only to be crushed by the Goth: and at the turning point of the Middle Ages, the liberty of Europe first asserted, the virtues of Christianity best practised, and its doctrines best attested, by a handful of mountain shepherds, without art, without literature, almost without a language, yet remaining unconquered in the midst of the Teutonic chivalry, and uncorrupted amidst the hierarchies of Rome. . . .

Now, therefore, the sum of all is, that you who wish to encourage Art in England have to do two things with it: you must delight in it, in the first place; and you must get it to serve some serious work, in the second place. I don't mean by serious, necessarily moral: all that I mean by serious is in some way or other useful, not merely selfish, careless, or indolent. I had, indeed, intended

before closing my address, to have traced out a few of
the directions in which, as it seems to me, Art may be
seriously and practically serviceable to us in the career
of civilization. I had hoped to show you how many of
the great phenomena of nature still remained unrecorded
by it, for us to record; how many of the historical
monuments of Europe were perishing without memorial, for the want of but a little honest, simple, laborious,
loving draughtsmanship; how many of the most impress-
ive historical events of the day failed of teaching us half
of what they were meant to teach, for want of painters
to represent them faithfully, instead of fancifully, and
with historical truth for their aim, instead of national
self-glorification. I had hoped to show you how many of
the best impulses of the heart were lost in frivolity or
sensuality, for want of purer beauty to contemplate,
and of noble thoughts to associate with the fervour of
hallowed human passion; how, finally, a great part of
the vital power of our religious faith was lost in us, for
want of such art as would realize in some rational,
probable, believable way, those events of sacred history
which, as they visibly and intelligibly occurred, may also
be visibly and intelligibly represented. But all this I dare
not do yet. I felt, as I thought over these things, that the
time was not yet come for their declaration: the time
will come for it, and I believe soon; but as yet, the man
would only lay himself open to the charge of vanity, of
imagination, and of idle fondness of hope, who should
venture to trace in words the course of the higher blessings which the Arts may have yet in store for mankind.
As yet there is no need to do so: all that we have to plead

for is an earnest and straightforward exertion in those courses of study which are opened to us day by day, believing only that they are to be followed gravely and for grave purposes, as by men, and not by children. I appeal, finally, to all those who are to become the pupils of these schools, to keep clear of the notion of following Art as dilettantism: it ought to delight you, as your reading delights you – but you never think of your reading as dilettantism. It ought to delight you as your studies of physical science delight you – but you don't call physical science dilettantism. If you are determined only to think of Art as a play or a pleasure, give it up at once: you will do no good to yourselves, and you will degrade the pursuit in the sight of others. Better, infinitely better, that you should never enter a picture gallery, than that you should enter only to saunter and to smile: better, infinitely better, that you should never handle a pencil at all, than handle it only for the sake of complacency in your small dexterity: better, infinitely better, that you should be wholly uninterested in pictures, and uninformed respecting them, than that you should just know enough to detect blemishes in great works, – to give a colour of reasonableness to presumption, and an appearance of acuteness to misunderstanding. Above all, I would plead for this so far as the teaching of these schools may be addressed to the junior Members of the University. Men employed in any kind of manual labour, by which they must live, are not likely to take up the notion that they can learn any other art for amusement only; but amateurs are: and it is of the highest importance, nay, it is just the one thing of all importance, to show them what drawing really means; and not so much to teach them to produce a good work themselves, as to know it when they see it done by others. Good work, in the stern sense of the word, as I before said, no mere amateur can do; and good work, in any sense, that is to say, profitable work for himself or for any one else, he can only do by being made in the beginning to see what is possible for him, and what not; – what is accessible, and what not; and by having the majesty and sternness of the everlasting laws of fact set before him in their infinitude. It is no matter for appalling him: the man is great already who is made well capable of being appalled; nor do we even wisely hope, nor truly understand, till we are humiliated by our hope, and awe-struck by our understanding. Nay, I will go farther than this, and say boldly, that what you have mainly to teach the young men here is, not so much what they can do, as what they cannot; – to make them see how much there is in nature which cannot be imitated, and how much in man which cannot be emulated. He only can be truly said to be educated in Art to whom all his work is only a feeble sign of glories which he cannot convey, and a feeble means of measuring, with ever-enlarging admiration, the great and untraversable gulf which God has set between the great and the common intelligences of mankind: and all the triumphs of Art which man can commonly achieve are only truly crowned by pure delight in natural scenes themselves, and by the sacred and self-forgetful veneration which can be nobly abashed, and tremblingly exalted, in the presence of a human spirit greater than his own.

Of Kings' Treasuries

'You shall each have a cake of sesame, – and ten pound.'
LUCIAN: *The Fisherman.*

My first duty this evening is to ask your pardon for the ambiguity of title under which the subject of lecture has been announced: for indeed I am not going to talk of kings, known as regnant, nor of treasuries, understood to contain wealth; but of quite another order of royalty, and another material of riches, than those usually acknowledged. I had even intended to ask your attention for a little while on trust, and (as sometimes one contrives, in taking a friend to see a favourite piece of scenery) to hide what I wanted most to show, with such imperfect cunning as I might, until we unexpectedly reached the best point of view by winding paths. But – and as also I have heard it said, by men practised in public address, that hearers are never so much fatigued as by the endeavour to follow a speaker who gives them no clue to his purpose, – I will take the slight mask off at once, and tell you plainly that I want to speak to you about the treasures hidden in books; and about the way we find them, and the way we lose them. A grave subject, you will say; and a wide one! Yes; so wide that I shall make no effort to touch the compass of it. I will try only to bring before you a few simple thoughts about reading, which press themselves upon me every day more deeply, as I watch the course of the public mind with respect to our daily enlarging means of education; and the answeringly wider spreading on the levels, of the irrigation of literature.

It happens that I have practically some connection with schools for different classes of youth; and I receive many letters from parents respecting the education of their children. In the mass of these letters I am always struck by the precedence which the idea of a 'position in life' takes above all other thoughts in the parents' – more especially in the mothers' – minds. 'The education befitting such and such a *station in life*' – this is the phrase, this the object, always. They never seek, as far as I can make out, an education good in itself; even the conception of abstract rightness in training rarely seems reached by the writers. But, an education 'which shall keep a good coat on my son's back; – which shall enable him to ring with confidence the visitors' bell at double-belled doors; which shall result ultimately in establishment of a double-belled door to his own house; – in a word, which shall lead to advancement in life; – *this* we pray for on bent knees – and this is *all* we pray for.' It never seems to occur to the parents that there may be an education which, in itself, *is* advancement in Life; – that any other than that may perhaps be advancement in Death; and that this essential education might be more easily got, or given, than they fancy, if they set about it in the right way; while it is for no price, and by no favour, to be got, if they set about it in the wrong.

Indeed, among the ideas most prevalent and effective

in the mind of this busiest of countries, I suppose the first – at least that which is confessed with the greatest frankness, and put forward as the fittest stimulus to youthful exertion – is this of 'Advancement in life.' May I ask you to consider with me, what this idea practically includes, and what it should include?

Practically, then, at present, 'advancement in life' means, becoming conspicuous in life; obtaining a position which shall be acknowledged by others to be respectable or honourable. We do not understand by this advancement, in general, the mere making of money, but the being known to have made it; not the accomplishment of any great aim, but the being seen to have accomplished it. In a word, we mean the gratification of our thirst for applause. That thirst, if the last infirmity of noble minds, is also the first infirmity of weak ones; and, on the whole, the strongest impulsive influence of average humanity: the greatest efforts of the race have always been traceable to the love of praise, as its greatest catastrophes to the love of pleasure.

I am not about to attack or defend this impulse. I want you only to feel how it lies at the root of effort; especially of all modern effort. It is the gratification of vanity which is, with us, the stimulus of toil and balm of repose; so closely does it touch the very springs of life that the wounding of our vanity is always spoken of (and truly) as in its measure *mortal*; we call it 'mortification,' using the same expression which we should apply to a gangrenous and incurable bodily hurt. And although a few of us may be physicans enough to recognize the various effect of this passion upon health and energy, I believe most honest men know, and would at once acknowledge, its leading power with them as a motive. The seaman does not commonly desire to be made captain only because he knows he can manage the ship better than any other sailor on board. He wants to be made captain that he may be *called* captain. The clergyman does not usually want to be made a bishop only because he believes that no other hand can, as firmly as his, direct the diocese through its difficulties. He wants to be made bishop primarily that he may be called 'My Lord.' And a prince does not usually desire to enlarge, or a subject to gain, a kingdom, because he believes no one else can as well serve the State, upon its throne; but, briefly, because he wishes to be addressed as 'Your Majesty,' by as many lips as may be brought to such utterance.

This, then, being the main idea of 'advancement in life,' the force of it applies, for all of us, according to our station, particularly to that secondary result of such advancement which we call 'getting into good society.' We want to get into good society, not that we may have it, but that we may be seen in it; and our notion of its goodness depends primarily on its conspicuousness.

Will you pardon me if I pause for a moment to put what I fear you may think an impertinent question? I never can go on with an address unless I feel, or know, that my audience are either with me or against me: I do not much care which, in beginning; but I must know where they are; and I would fain find out, at this instant, whether you think I am putting the motives of popular action too low. I am resolved, to-night, to state them low enough to be admitted as probable; for whenever, in my writings on Political Economy, I assume that a little honesty, or generosity, – or what used to be called 'virtue,' – may be calculated upon as a human motive of action, people always answer me, saying, 'You must not calculate on that: that is not in human nature: you must not assume anything to be common to men but acquisitiveness and jealousy; no other feeling ever has influence on them, except accidentally, and in matters out of the way of business.' I begin, accordingly, to-night low in the scale of motives; but I must know if you think me right in doing so. Therefore, let me ask those who admit the love of praise to be usually the strongest motive in men's minds in seeking advancement, and the honest desire of doing any kind of duty to be an entirely secondary one, to hold up their hands. (*About a dozen hands held up – the audience, partly, not being sure the lecturer is serious, and, partly, shy of expressing opinion.*) I am quite serious – I really do want to know what you think; however, I can judge by putting the reverse question. Will those who think that duty is generally the first, and love of praise the second motive, hold up their hands? (*One hand reported to have been held up behind the lecturer.*) Very good: I see you are with me, and that you think I have not begun too near the ground. Now, without teasing you by putting farther question, I venture to assume that you will admit duty as at least a secondary or tertiary motive. You think that the desire of doing something useful, or obtaining some real good, is indeed an existent collateral idea, though a secondary one, in most men's desire of advancement. You will grant that moderately honest men desire place and office, at least in some measure for the sake of beneficent power; and would wish to associate rather with sensible and well-informed persons than with fools and ignorant persons, whether they are seen in the company of the sensible ones or not. And finally, without being troubled by repetition of any common truisms about the preciousness of friends, and the influence of companions, you will admit, doubtless, that according to the sincerity of our desire that our friends may be true, and our companions wise, – and in proportion to the earnestness and discretion with which we choose both, – will be the general chances of our happiness and usefulness.

But, granting that we had both the will and the sense to choose our friends well, how few of us have the power! or, at least, how limited, for most, is the sphere of choice! Nearly all our associations are determined by chance or necessity; and restricted within a narrow circle. We cannot know whom we would; and those whom we know, we cannot have at our side when we most need them. All the higher circles of human intelligence are, to those beneath, only momentarily and partially open. We may, by good fortune, obtain a glimpse of a great poet, and hear the sound of his voice; or put a question to a man of science, and be answered good-humouredly. We may intrude ten minutes' talk on a cabinet minister, answered probably with words worse than silence, being deceptive; or snatch, once or twice in our lives, the privilege of throwing a bouquet in the path of a princess, or arresting the kind glance of a queen. And yet these momentary chances we covet; and spend our years, and passions, and powers, in pursuit of little more than these;

while, meantime, there is a society continually open to us, of people who will talk to us as long as we like, whatever our rank or occupation; – talk to us in the best words they can choose, and of the things nearest their hearts. And this society, because it is so numerous and so gentle, and can be kept waiting round us all day long, – kings and statesmen lingering patiently, not to grant audience, but to gain it! – in those plainly furnished and narrow ante-rooms, our bookcase shelves, – we make no account of that company, – perhaps never listen to a word they would say, all day long!

You may tell me, perhaps, or think within yourselves, that the apathy with which we regard this company of the noble, who are praying us to listen to them; and the passion with which we pursue the company, probably of the ignoble, who despise us, or who have nothing to teach us, are grounded in this, – that we can see the faces of the living men, and it is themselves, and not their sayings, with which we desire to become familiar. But it is not so. Suppose you never were to see their faces; – suppose you could be put behind a screen in the states-man's cabinet, or the prince's chamber, would you not be glad to listen to their words, though you were forbidden to advance beyond the screen? And when the screen is only a little less, folded in two instead of four, and you can be hidden behind the cover of the two boards that bind a book, and listen all day long, not to the casual talk, but to the studied, determined, chosen addresses of the wisest of men; – this station of audience, and honourable privy council, you despise!

But perhaps you will say that it is because the living

people talk of things that are passing, and are of immediate interest to you, that you desire to hear them. Nay; that cannot be so, for the living people will themselves tell you about passing matters much better in their writings than in their careless talk. Yet I admit that this motive does influence you, so far as you prefer those rapid and ephemeral writings to slow and enduring writings – books, properly so called. For all books are divisible into two classes, the books of the hour, and the books of all time. Mark this distinction – it is not one of quality only. It is not merely the bad book that does not last, and the good one that does. It is a distinction of species. There are good books for the hour, and good ones for all time; bad books for the hour, and bad ones for all time. I must define the two kinds before I go farther.

The good book of the hour, then, – I do not speak of the bad ones, – is simply the useful or pleasant talk of some person whom you cannot otherwise converse with, printed for you. Very useful often, telling you what you need to know; very pleasant often, as a sensible friend's present talk would be. These bright accounts of travels; good-humoured and witty discussions of question; lively or pathetic story-telling in the form of novel; firm fact-telling, by the real agents concerned in the events of passing history; – all these books of the hour, multiplying among us as education becomes more general, are a peculiar possession of the present age: we ought to be entirely thankful for them, and entirely ashamed of ourselves if we make no good use of them. But we make the worst possible use if we allow them to usurp the place of true books: for, strictly speaking, they are not books at all, but merely letters or newspapers in good print. Our friend's letter may be delightful, or necessary, to-day: whether worth keeping or not, is to be considered. The newspaper may be entirely proper at breakfast time, but assuredly it is not reading for all day. So, though bound up in a volume, the long letter which gives you so pleasant an account of the inns, and roads, and weather, last year at such a place, or which tells you that amusing story, or gives you the real circumstances of such and such events, however valuable for occasional reference, may not be, in the real sense of the word, a 'book' at all, nor, in the real sense, to be 'read.' A book is essentially not a talking thing, but a written thing; and written, not with a view of mere communication, but of permanence. The book of talk is printed only because its author cannot speak to thousands of people at once; if he could, he would – the volume is mere *multiplication* of his voice. You cannot talk to your friend in India; if you could, you would; you write instead: that is mere *conveyance* of voice. But a book is written, not to multiply the voice merely, not to carry it merely, but to perpetuate it. The author has something to say which he perceives to be true and useful, or helpfully beautiful. So far as he knows, no one has yet said it; so far as he knows, no one else can say it. He is bound to say it, clearly and melodiously if he may; clearly at all events. In the sum of his life he finds this to be the thing, or group of things, manifest to him; – this, the piece of true knowledge, or sight, which his share of sunshine and earth has permitted him to seize. He would fain set it down for ever; engrave it on rock, if he could; saying, 'This is the best of me; for the rest, I ate, and drank, and slept, loved, and hated, like another; my life was as the vapour, and is not; but this I saw and knew: this, if anything of mine, is worth your memory.' That is his 'writing'; it is, in his small human way, and with whatever degree of true inspiration is in him, his inscription, or scripture. That is a 'Book.'

Perhaps you think no books were ever so written?

But, again, I ask you, do you at all believe in honesty, or at all in kindness, or do you think there is never any honesty or benevolence in wise people? None of us, I hope, are so unhappy as to think that. Well, whatever bit of a wise man's work is honestly and benevolently done, that bit is his book or his piece of art. It is mixed always with evil fragments – ill-done, redundant, affected work. But if you read rightly, you will easily discover the true bits, and those *are* the book.

Now books of this kind have been written in all ages by their greatest men: – by great leaders, great statesmen, and great thinkers. These are all at your choice; and Life is short. You have heard as much before; – yet have you measured and mapped out this short life and its possibilities? Do you know, if you read this, that you cannot read that – that what you lose to-day you cannot gain to-morrow? Will you go and gossip with your housemaid, or your stable-boy, when you may talk with queens and kings; or flatter yourself that it is with any worthy consciousness of your own claims to respect, that you jostle with the hungry and common crowd for *entrée* here, and audience there, when all the while this eternal court is open to you, with its society, wide as the world, multitudinous as its days, the chosen, and the mighty, of every place and time? Into that you may enter always; in that you may take fellowship and rank according to your wish; from that, once entered into it, you can never be outcast but by your own fault; by your aristocracy of companionship there, your own inherent aristocracy will be assuredly tested, and the motives with which you strive to take high place in the society of the living, measured, as to all the truth and sincerity that are in them, by the place you desire to take in this company of the Dead.

'The place you desire,' and the place you *fit yourself for*, I must also say; because, observe, this court of the past differs from all living aristocracy in this: – it is open to labour and to merit, but to nothing else. No wealth will bribe, no name overawe, no artifice deceive, the guardian of those Elysian gates. In the deep sense, no vile or vulgar person ever enters there. At the portières of that silent Faubourg St Germain, there is but brief question: – 'Do you deserve to enter? Pass. Do you ask to be the companion of nobles? Make yourself noble, and you shall be. Do you long for the conversation of the wise? Learn to understand it, and you shall hear it. But on other terms? – no. If you will not rise to us, we cannot stoop to you. The living lord may assume courtesy, the living philosopher explain his thought to you with considerate pain; but here we neither feign nor interpret; you must rise to the level of our thoughts if you would be gladdened by them, and share our feelings, if you would recognize our presence.'

This, then, is what you have to do, and I admit that it

is much. You must, in a word, love these people, if you are to be among them. No ambition is of any use. They scorn your ambition. You must love them, and show your love in these two following ways.

(1) First, by a true desire to be taught by them, and to enter into their thoughts. To enter into theirs, observe; not to find your own expressed by them. If the person who wrote the book is not wiser than you, you need not read it; if he be, he will think differently from you in many respects.

(2) Very ready we are to say of a book, 'How good this is – that's exactly what I think!' But the right feeling is, 'How strange that is! I never thought of that before, and yet I see it is true; or if I do not now, I hope I shall, some day.' But whether thus submissively or not, at least be sure that you go to the author to get at *his* meaning, not to find yours. Judge it afterwards if you think yourself qualified to do so; but ascertain it first. And be sure, also, if the author is worth anything, that you will not get at his meaning all at once; – nay, that at his whole meaning you will not for a long time arrive in any wise. Not that he does not say what he means, and in strong words too; but he cannot say it all; and what is more strange, *will* not, but in a hidden way and in parables, in order that he may be sure you want it. I cannot quite see the reason of this, nor analyse that cruel reticence in the breasts of wise men which makes them always hide their deeper thought. They do not give it you by way of help, but of reward; and will make themselves sure that you deserve it before they allow you to reach it. But it is the same with the physical type of wisdom, gold. There seems, to

you and me, no reason why the electric forces of the earth should not carry whatever there is of gold within it at once to the mountain tops, so that kings and people might know that all the gold they could get was there; and without any trouble of digging, or anxiety, or chance, or waste of time, cut it away, and coin as much as they needed. But Nature does not manage it so. She puts it in little fissures in the earth, nobody knows where: you may dig long and find none; you must dig painfully to find any.

And it is just the same with men's best wisdom. When you come to a good book, you must ask yourself, 'Am I inclined to work as an Australian miner would? Are my pickaxes and shovels in good order, and am I in good trim myself, my sleeves well up to the elbow, and my breath good, and my temper?' And, keeping the figure a little longer, even at cost of tiresomeness, for it is a thoroughly useful one, the metal you are in search of being the author's mind or meaning, his words are as the rock which you have to crush and smelt in order to get at it. And your pickaxes are your own care, wit, and learning; your smelting furnace is your own thoughtful soul. Do not hope to get at any good author's meaning without those tools and that fire; often you will need sharpest, finest chiselling, and patientest fusing, before you can gather one grain of the metal.

And, therefore, first of all, I tell you earnestly and authoritatively (I *know* I am right in this), you must get into the habit of looking intensely at words, and assuring yourself of their meaning, syllable by syllable – nay, letter by letter. For though it is only by reason of the opposition of letters in the function of signs, to sounds in the function of signs, that the study of books is called 'literature,' and that a man versed in it is called, by the consent of nations, a man of letters instead of a man of books, or of words, you may yet connect with that accidental nomenclature this real fact: – that you might read all the books in the British Museum (if you could live long enough), and remain an utterly 'illiterate,' uneducated person; but that if you read ten pages of a good book, letter by letter, – that is to say, with real accuracy, – you are for evermore in some measure an educated person. The entire difference between education and non-education (as regards the merely intellectual part of it), consists in this accuracy. A well-educated gentleman may not know many languages, – may not be able to speak any but his own, – may have read very few books. But whatever language he knows, he knows precisely; whatever word he pronounces, he pronounces rightly; above all, he is learned in the *peerage* of words; knows the words of true descent and ancient blood, at a glance, from words of modern canaille; remembers all their ancestry, their intermarriages, distant relationships, and the extent to which they were admitted, and offices they held, among the national noblesse of words at any time, and in any country. But an uneducated person may know, by memory, many languages, and talk them all, and yet truly know not a word of any, – not a word even of his own. An ordinarily clever and sensible seaman will be able to make his way ashore at most ports; yet he has only to speak a sentence of any language to be known for an illiterate person: so also the accent, or turn of expression of a single sentence, will at once mark a scholar. And this is so strongly felt, so conclusively admitted, by educated persons, that a false accent or a mistaken syllable is enough, in the parliament of any civilized nation, to assign to a man a certain degree of inferior standing for ever.

And this is right; but it is a pity that the accuracy insisted on is not greater, and required to a serious purpose. It is right that a false Latin quantity should excite a smile in the House of Commons; but it is wrong that a false English *meaning* should *not* excite a frown there. Let the accent of words be watched; and closely: let their meaning be watched more closely still, and fewer will do the work. A few words well chosen, and distinguished, will do work that a thousand cannot, when every one is acting, equivocally, in the function of another. Yes; and words, if they are not watched, will do deadly work sometimes. There are masked words droning and skulking about us in Europe just now, – (there never were so many, owing to the spread of a shallow, blotching, blundering, infectious 'information,' or rather deformation, everywhere, and to the teaching of catechisms and phrases at school instead of human meanings) – there are masked words abroad, I say, which nobody understands, but which everybody uses, and most people will also fight for, live for, or even die for, fancying they mean this or that, or the other, of things dear to them: for such words wear chameleon cloaks – 'ground-lion' cloaks, of the colour of the ground of any man's fancy: on that ground they lie in wait, and rend them with a spring from it. There never were creatures of prey so mischievous, never diplomatists so cunning, never poisoners so deadly, as these masked words; they are the unjust stewards of all men's ideas: whatever fancy or favourite instinct a man most cherishes, he gives to his favourite masked word to take care of for him; the word at last comes to have an infinite power over him, – you cannot get at him but by its ministry.

And in languages so mongrel in breed as the English, there is a fatal power of equivocation put into men's hands, almost whether they will or no, in being able to use Greek or Latin words for an idea when they want it to be awful; and Saxon or otherwise common words when they want it to be vulgar. What a singular and salutary effect, for instance, would be produced on the minds of people who are in the habit of taking the Form of the 'Word' they live by, for the Power of which that Word tells them, if we always either retained, or refused, the Greek form 'biblos,' or 'biblion,' as the right expression for 'book' – instead of employing it only in the one instance in which we wish to give dignity to the idea, and translating it into English everywhere else. How wholesome it would be for many simple persons if, in such places (for instance) as Acts xix.19, we retained the Greek expression, instead of translating it, and they had to read – 'Many of them also which used curious arts, brought their bibles together, and burnt them before all men; and they counted the price of them, and found it fifty thousand pieces of silver'! Or if, on the other hand, we translated where we retain it, and always spoke of 'The Holy Book,' instead of 'Holy Bible,' it might come into more heads than it does at present, that the Word of God, by which the heavens were, of old, and by which they are now kept in store,[1] cannot be made a present of to anybody in morocco binding; nor sown on any wayside by help either of steam plough or steam press; but is nevertheless being offered to us daily, and by us with contumely refused; and sown in us daily, and by us, as instantly as may be, choked.

So, again, consider what effect has been produced on the English vulgar mind by the use of the sonorous Latin form 'damno,' in translating the Greek κατακρίνω, when people charitably wish to make it forcible; and the substitution of the temperate 'condemn' for it, when they choose to keep it gentle; and what notable sermons have been preached by illiterate clergymen on – 'He that believeth not shall be damned'; though they would shrink with horror from translating Heb. xi.7, 'The saving of his house, by which he damned the world,' or John viii.10–11, 'Woman, hath no man damned thee? She saith, No man, Lord. Jesus answered her, Neither do I damn thee: go and sin no more.' And divisions in the mind of Europe, which have cost seas of blood, and in the defence of which the noblest souls of men have been cast away in frantic desolation, countless as forest-leaves – though, in the heart of them, founded on deeper causes – have nevertheless been rendered practically possible, mainly, by the European adoption of the Greek word for a public meeting, 'ecclesia,' to give peculiar respectability to such meetings, when held for religious purposes; and other collateral equivocations, such as the vulgar English one of using the word 'priest' as a contraction for 'presbyter.'

Now, in order to deal with words rightly, this is the

habit you must form. Nearly every word in your language has been first a word of some other language – of Saxon, German, French, Latin, or Greek; (not to speak of eastern and primitive dialects). And many words have been all these – that is to say, have been Greek first, Latin next, French or German next, and English last: undergoing a certain change of sense and use on the lips of each nation; but retaining a deep vital meaning, which all good scholars feel in employing them, even at this day. If you do not know the Greek alphabet, learn it; young or old – girl or boy – whoever you may be, if you think of reading seriously (which, of course, implies that you have some leisure at command), learn your Greek alphabet; then get good dictionaries of all these languages, and whenever you are in doubt about a word, hunt it down patiently. Read Max Müller's lectures thoroughly, to begin with; and, after that, never let a word escape you that looks suspicious. It is severe work; but you will find it, even at first, interesting, and at last endlessly amusing. And the general gain to your character, in power and precision, will be quite incalculable.

Mind, this does not imply knowing, or trying to know, Greek or Latin, or French. It takes a whole life to learn any language perfectly. But you can easily ascertain the meanings through which the English word has passed; and those which in a good writer's work it must still bear.

And now, merely for example's sake, I will, with your permission, read a few lines of a true book with you, carefully; and see what will come out of them. I will take a book perfectly known to you all. No English words are more familiar to us, yet few perhaps have been read with

less sincerity. I will take these few following lines of
Lycidas: –

> 'Last came, and last did go,
> The pilot of the Galilean lake.
> Two massy keys he bore of metals twain,
> (The golden opes, the iron shuts amain,)
> He shook his mitred locks, and stern bespake,
> "How well could I have spared for thee, young swain,
> Enow of such as for their bellies' sake
> Creep, and intrude, and climb into the fold!
> Of other care they little reckoning make,
> Than how to scramble at the shearers' feast,
> And shove away the worthy bidden guest;
> Blind mouths! that scarce themselves know how to hold
> A sheep-hook, or have learn'd aught else, the least
> That to the faithful herdman's art belongs!
> What recks it them? What need they? They are sped;
> And when they list, their lean and flashy songs
> Grate on their scrannel pipes of wretched straw;
> The hungry sheep look up, and are not fed,
> But, swoln with wind, and the rank mist they draw,
> Rot inwardly, and foul contagion spread;
> Besides what the grim wolf with privy paw
> Daily devours apace, and nothing said.'

Let us think over this passage, and examine its words.
First, is it not singular to find Milton assigning to
St Peter, not only his full episcopal function, but the
very types of it which Protestants usually refuse most
passionately? His 'mitred' locks! Milton was no Bishop-

lover; how comes St Peter to be 'mitred'? 'Two massy
keys he bore.' Is this, then, the power of the keys claimed
by the Bishops of Rome? and is it acknowledged here by
Milton only in a poetical licence, for the sake of its
picturesqueness, that he may get the gleam of the golden
keys to help his effect?

Do not think it. Great men do not play stage tricks
with the doctrines of life and death: only little men do
that. Milton means what he says; and means it with his
might too – is going to put the whole strength of his
spirit presently into the saying of it. For though not a
lover of false bishops, he *was* a lover of true ones; and
the Lake-pilot is here, in his thoughts, the type and head
of true episcopal power. For Milton reads that text, 'I
will give unto thee the keys of the kingdom of heaven,'
quite honestly. Puritan though he be, he would not blot
it out of the book because there have been bad bishops;
nay, in order to understand *him*, we must understand
that verse first; it will not do to eye it askance, or whisper
it under our breath, as if it were a weapon of an adverse
sect. It is a solemn, universal assertion, deeply to be kept
in mind by all sects. But perhaps we shall be better able
to reason on it if we go on a little farther, and come back
to it. For clearly this marked insistence on the power of
the true episcopate is to make us feel more weightily
what is to be charged against the false claimants of
episcopate; or generally, against false claimants of power
and rank in the body of the clergy; they who, 'for their
bellies' sake, creep, and intrude, and climb into the fold.'

Never think Milton uses those three words to fill up
his verse, as a loose writer would. He needs all the three;

– especially those three, and no more than those – 'creep,' and 'intrude,' and 'climb'; no other words would or could serve the turn, and no more could be added. For they exhaustively comprehend the three classes, correspondent to the three characters, of men who dishonestly seek ecclesiastical power. First, those who *'creep'* into the fold; who do not care for office, nor name, but for secret influence, and do all things occultly and cunningly, consenting to any servility of office or conduct, so only that they may intimately discern, and unawares direct, the minds of men. Then those who 'intrude' (thrust, that is) themselves into the fold, who by natural insolence of heart, and stout eloquence of tongue, and fearlessly perseverant self-assertion, obtain hearing and authority with the common crowd. Lastly, those who 'climb,' who, by labour and learning, both stout and sound, but selfishly exerted in the cause of their own ambition, gain high dignities and authorities, and become 'lords over the heritage,' though not 'ensamples to the flock.'

Now go on: –

> 'Of other care they little reckoning make,
> Than how to scramble at the shearers' feast.
> *Blind mouths –*'

I pause again, for this is a strange expression; a broken metaphor, one might think, careless and unscholarly.

Not so: its very audacity and pithiness are intended to make us look close at the phrase and remember it. Those two monosyllables express the precisely accurate contraries of right character, in the two great offices of the Church – those of bishop and pastor.

A 'Bishop' means 'a person who sees.'

A 'Pastor' means 'a person who feeds.'

The most unbishoply character a man can have is therefore to be Blind.

The most unpastoral is, instead of feeding, to want to be fed, – to be a Mouth.

Take the two reverses together, and you have 'blind mouths.' We may advisably follow out this idea a little. Nearly all the evils in the Church have arisen from bishops desiring *power* more than *light*. They want authority, not outlook. Whereas their real office is not to rule; though it may be vigorously to exhort and rebuke: it is the king's office to rule; the bishop's office is to *oversee* the flock; to number it, sheep by sheep; to be ready always to give full account of it. Now it is clear he cannot give account of the souls, if he has not so much as numbered the bodies, of his flock. The first thing, therefore, that a bishop has to do is at least to put himself in a position in which, at any moment, he can obtain the history, from childhood, of every living soul in his diocese, and of its present state. Down in that back street, Bill and Nancy, knocking each other's teeth out! – Does the bishop know all about it? Has he his eye upon them? Has he *had* his eye upon them? Can he circumstantially explain to us how Bill got into the habit of beating Nancy about the head? If he cannot, he is no bishop, though he had a mitre as high as Salisbury steeple; he is no bishop, – he has sought to be at the helm instead of the mast-head; he has no sight of things. 'Nay,' you say, 'it is not his duty to look after Bill in the back street.' What! the fat sheep that have full fleeces – you think it is only those he should look after while (go back to your Milton) 'the hungry sheep look up, and are not fed, besides what the grim wolf, with privy paw' (bishops knowing nothing about it), 'daily devours apace, and nothing said'?

'But that's not our idea of a bishop.' Perhaps not; but it was St Paul's; and it was Milton's. They may be right, or we may be; but we must not think we are reading either one or the other by putting our meaning into their words.

I go on.

'But swoln with wind, and the rank mist they draw.'

This is to meet the vulgar answer that 'if the poor are not looked after in their bodies, they are in their souls; they have spiritual food.'

And Milton says, 'They have no such thing as spiritual food; they are only swollen with wind.' At first you may think that is a coarse type, and an obscure one. But again, it is a quite literally accurate one. Take up your Latin and Greek dictionaries, and find out the meaning of 'Spirit.' It is only a contraction of the Latin word 'breath,' and an indistinct translation of the Greek word for 'wind.' The same word is used in writing, 'The wind bloweth where it listeth'; and in writing, 'So is every one that is born of the Spirit'; born of the *breath*, that is; for it means the breath of God, in soul and body. We have the true sense of it in our words 'inspiration' and 'expire.' Now, there are two kinds of breath with which the flock may be filled, – God's breath, and man's. The breath of God is health, and life, and peace to them, as the air of heaven is to the flocks on the hills; but man's breath – the word which *he* calls spiritual – is disease and contagion to them, as the fog of the fen. They rot inwardly with it; they are puffed up by it, as a dead body by the vapours of its own decomposition. This is literally true of all false religious teaching; the first and last, and fatalest sign of it, is that 'puffing up.' Your converted children, who teach their parents; your converted convicts, who teach honest men; your converted dunces, who, having lived in cretinous stupefaction half their lives, suddenly awaking to the fact of there being a God, fancy themselves therefore His peculiar people and messengers; your sectarians of every species, small and great, Catholic or Protestant, of high church or low, in so far as they think themselves exclusively in the right and others wrong; and, pre-eminently, in every sect, those who hold that men can be saved by thinking rightly instead of doing rightly, by word instead of act, and wish instead of work; – these are the true fog children – clouds, these, without water; bodies, these, of putrescent vapour and skin, without blood or flesh: blown bagpipes for the fiends to pipe with – corrupt, and corrupting, – 'Swollen with wind, and the rank mist they draw.'

Lastly, let us return to the lines respecting the power of the keys, for now we can understand them. Note the difference between Milton and Dante in their interpretation of this power: for once, the latter is weaker in thought; he supposes *both* the keys to be of the gate of heaven; one is of gold, the other of silver: they are given by St Peter to the sentinel angel; and it is not easy to determine the meaning either of the substances of the three steps of the gate, or of the two keys. But Milton makes one, of gold, the key of heaven; the other, of iron, the key of the prison in which the wicked teachers are to be bound who 'have taken away the key of knowledge, yet entered not in themselves.'

We have seen that the duties of bishop and pastor are to see, and feed; and of all who do so it is said, 'He that watereth, shall be watered also himself.' But the reverse is truth also. He that watereth not, shall be *withered* himself; and he that seeth not, shall himself be shut out of sight – shut into the perpetual prison-house. And that prison opens here, as well as hereafter: he who is to be bound in heaven must first be bound on earth. That command to the strong angels, of which the rock-apostle is the image, 'Take him, and bind him hand and foot, and cast him out,' issues, in its measure, against the teacher, for every help withheld, and for every truth refused, and for every falsehood enforced; so that he is more strictly fettered the more he fetters, and farther outcast as he more and more misleads, till at last the bars of the iron cage close upon him, and as 'the golden opes, the iron shuts amain.'

We have got something out of the lines, I think, and much more is yet to be found in them; but we have done enough by way of example of the kind of word-by-word examination of your author which is rightly called 'reading'; watching every accent and expression, and putting ourselves always in the author's place, annihilating our own personality, and seeking to enter into his, so as to be able assuredly to say, 'Thus Milton thought,' not 'Thus *I* thought, in mis-reading Milton.' And by this process you will gradually come to attach less weight to your own 'Thus I thought' at other times. You will begin to perceive that what *you* thought was a matter of no serious importance; – that your thoughts on any subject are not perhaps the clearest and wisest that could be arrived at thereupon: – in fact, that unless you are a very singular person, you cannot be said to have any 'thoughts' at all; that you have no materials for them, in any serious matters;[2] – no right to 'think,' but only to try to learn more of the facts. Nay, most probably all your life (unless, as I said, you are a singular person) you will have no legitimate right to an 'opinion' on any business, except that instantly under your hand. What must of necessity be done, you can always find out, beyond question, how to do. Have you a house to keep in order, a commodity to sell, a field to plough, a ditch to cleanse? There need be no two opinions about these proceedings; it is at your peril if you have not much more than an 'opinion' on the way to manage such matters. And also, outside of your own business, there are one or two subjects on which you are bound to have but one opinion. That roguery and lying are objection-able, and are instantly to be flogged out of the way whenever discovered; – that covetousness and love of quarrelling are dangerous dispositions even in children, and deadly dispositions in men and nations; – that, in the end, the God of heaven and earth loves active, modest, and kind people, and hates idle, proud, greedy, and cruel ones; – on these general facts you are bound to have but one, and that a very strong, opinion. For the rest, respecting religions, governments, sciences, arts, you will find that, on the whole, you can know NOTHING, – judge nothing; that the best you can do, even though you may be a well-educated person, is to be silent, and strive to be wiser every day, and to understand a little more of the thoughts of others, which so soon as you try to do honestly, you will discover that the thoughts even of the wisest are very little more than pertinent questions. To put the difficulty into a clear shape, and exhibit to you the grounds for *in*decision, that is all they can generally do for you! – and well for them and for us, if indeed they are able 'to mix the music with our thoughts and sadden us with heavenly doubts.' This writer, from whom I have been reading to you, is not among the first or wisest: he sees shrewdly as far as he sees, and therefore it is easy to find out its full meaning; but with the greater men, you cannot fathom their meaning; they do not even wholly measure it them-selves, – it is so wide. Suppose I had asked you, for instance, to seek for Shakespeare's opinion, instead of Milton's, on this matter of Church authority? – or for Dante's? Have any of you, at this instant, the least idea what either thought about it? Have you ever balanced the scene with the bishops in *Richard III* against the character of Cranmer? the description of St Francis and St Dominic against that of him who made Virgil wonder to gaze upon him, – 'disteso, tanto vilmente, nell' eterno esilio': or of him whom Dante stood beside, 'come 'l frate che confessa lo perfido assassin'? Shakespeare and Alighieri knew men better than most of us, I presume!

They were both in the midst of the main struggle between the temporal and spiritual powers. They had an opinion, we may guess. But where is it? Bring it into court! Put Shakespeare's or Dante's creed into articles, and send *it* up for trial by the Ecclesiastical Courts!

You will not be able, I tell you again, for many and many a day, to come at the real purposes and teaching of these great men; but a very little honest study of them will enable you to perceive that what you took for your own 'judgment' was mere chance prejudice, and drifted, helpless, entangled weed of castaway thought; nay, you will see that most men's minds are indeed little better than rough heath wilderness, neglected and stubborn, partly barren, partly overgrown with pestilent brakes, and venomous, wind-sown herbage of evil surmise; that the first thing you have to do for them, and yourself, is eagerly and scornfully to set fire to *this*; burn all the jungle into wholesome ash-heaps, and then plough and sow. All the true literary work before you, for life, must begin with obedience to that order, 'Break up your fallow ground, and *sow not among thorns.*'

(II.) Having then faithfully listened to the great teachers, that you may enter into their Thoughts, you have yet this higher advance to make; – you have to enter into their Hearts. As you go to them first for clear sight, so you must stay with them, that you may share at last their just and mighty Passion. Passion, or 'sensation.' I am not afraid of the word; still less of the thing. You have heard many outcries against sensation lately; but, I can tell you, it is not less sensation we want, but more. The ennobling difference between one man and another, – between one animal and another, – is precisely in this, that one feels more than another. If we were sponges, perhaps sensation might not be easily got for us; if we were earth-worms, liable at every instant to be cut in two by the spade, perhaps too much sensation might not be good for us. But being human creatures, it *is* good for us; nay, we are only human in so far as we are sensitive, and our honour is precisely in proportion to our passion.

You know I said of that great and pure society of the Dead, that it would allow 'no vain or vulgar person to enter there.' What do you think I meant by a 'vulgar' person? What do you yourselves mean by 'vulgarity'? You will find it a fruitful subject of thought; but, briefly, the essence of all vulgarity lies in want of sensation. Simple and innocent vulgarity is merely an untrained and undeveloped bluntness of body and mind; but in true inbred vulgarity, there is a dreadful callousness, which, in extremity, becomes capable of every sort of bestial habit and crime, without fear, without pleasure, without horror, and without pity. It is in the blunt hand and the dead heart, in the diseased habit, in the hardened conscience, that men become vulgar; they are for ever vulgar, precisely in proportion as they are incapable of sympathy, – of quick understanding, – of all that, in deep insistence on the common, but most accurate term, may be called the 'tact' or 'touch-faculty,' of body and soul: that tact which the Mimosa has in trees, which the pure woman has above all creatures; – fineness and fulness of sensation, beyond reason; – the guide and sanctifier of reason itself. Reason can but determine what is true: – it

65

is the God-given passion of humanity which alone can recognize what God has made good.

We come then to that great concourse of the Dead, not merely to know from them what is True, but chiefly to feel with them what is just. Now, to feel with them, we must be like them; and none of us can become that without pains. As the true knowledge is disciplined and tested knowledge, – not the first thought that comes, so the true passion is disciplined and tested passion, – not the first passion that comes. The first that come are the vain, the false, the treacherous; if you yield to them they will lead you wildly and far, in vain pursuit, in hollow enthusiasm, till you have no true purpose and no true passion left. Not that any feeling possible to humanity is in itself wrong, but only wrong when undisciplined. Its nobility is in its force and justice; it is wrong when it is weak, and felt for paltry cause. There is a mean wonder, as of a child who sees a juggler tossing golden balls; and this is base, if you will. But do you think that the wonder is ignoble, or the sensation less, with which every human soul is called to watch the golden balls of heaven tossed through the night by the Hand that made them? There is a mean curiosity, as of a child opening a forbidden door, or a servant prying into her master's business; – and a noble curiosity, questioning, in the front of danger, the source of the great river beyond the sand, – the place of the great continents beyond the sea; – a nobler curiosity still, which questions of the source of the River of Life, and of the space of the Continent of Heaven, – things which 'the angels desire to look into.' So the anxiety is ignoble, with which you linger over the course

and catastrophe of an idle tale; but do you think the
anxiety is less, or greater, with which you watch, or
ought to watch, the dealings of fate and destiny with the
life of an agonized nation? Alas! it is the narrowness,
selfishness, minuteness, of your sensation that you have
to deplore in England at this day; – sensation which
spends itself in bouquets and speeches: in revellings and
junketings; in sham fights and gay puppet shows, while
you can look on and see noble nations murdered, man
by man, without an effort or a tear.

I said 'minuteness' and 'selfishness' of sensation, but
it would have been enough to have said 'injustice' or
'unrighteousness' of sensation. For as in nothing is a
gentleman better to be discerned from a vulgar person,
so in nothing is a gentle nation (such nations have been)
better to be discerned from a mob, than in this, – that
their feelings are constant and just, results of due contemplation, and of equal thought. You can talk a mob into
anything; its feelings may be – usually are – on the whole,
generous and right; but it has no foundation for them,
no hold of them; you may tease or tickle it into any, at
your pleasure; it thinks by infection, for the most part,
catching an opinion like a cold, and there is nothing so
little that it will not roar itself wild about, when the fit
is on; – nothing so great but it will forget in an hour,
when the fit is past. But a gentleman's, or a gentle
nation's, passions are just, measured, and continuous.
A great nation, for instance, does not spend its entire
national wits for a couple of months in weighing
evidence of a single ruffian's having done a single murder; and for a couple of years see its own children murder

each other by their thousands or tens of thousands a day, considering only what the effect is likely to be on the price of cotton, and caring no wise to determine which side of battle is in the wrong. Neither does a great nation send its poor little boys to jail for stealing six walnuts; and allow its bankrupts to steal their hundreds of thousands with a bow, and its bankers, rich with poor men's savings, to close their doors 'under circumstances over which they have no control,' with a 'by your leave'; and large landed estates to be bought by men who have made their money by going with armed steamers up and down the China Seas, selling opium at the cannon's mouth, and altering, for the benefit of the foreign nation, the common highwayman's demand of 'your money *or* your life,' into that of 'your money *and* your life.' Neither does a great nation allow the lives of its innocent poor to be parched out of them by fog fever, and rotted out of them by dunghill plague, for the sake of sixpence a life extra per week to its landlords; and then debate, with drivelling tears, and diabolical sympathies, whether it ought not piously to save, and nursingly cherish, the lives of its murderers. Also, a great nation having made up its mind that hanging is quite the wholesomest process for its homicides in general, can yet with mercy distinguish between the degrees of guilt in homicides; and does not yelp like a pack of frost-pinched wolf-cubs on the blood-track of an unhappy crazed boy, or grey-haired clodpate Othello, 'perplexed i' the extreme,' at the very moment that it is sending a Minister of the Crown to make polite speeches to a man who is bayoneting young girls in their fathers' sight, and killing noble youths in cool blood, faster than a country butcher kills lambs in spring. And, lastly, a great nation does not mock Heaven and its Powers, by pretending belief in a revelation which asserts the love of money to be the root of *all* evil, and declaring, at the same time, that it is actuated, and intends to be actuated, in all chief national deeds and measures, by no other love.

My friends, I do not know why any of us should talk about reading. We want some sharper discipline than that of reading; but, at all events, be assured, we cannot read. No reading is possible for a people with its mind in this state. No sentence of any great writer is intelligible to them. It is simply and sternly impossible for the English public, at this moment, to understand any thoughtful writing, – so incapable of thought has it become in its insanity of avarice. Happily, our disease is, as yet, little worse than this incapacity of thought; it is not corruption of the inner nature; we ring true still, when anything strikes home to us; and though the idea that everything should 'pay' has infected our every purpose so deeply, that even when we would play the good Samaritan, we never take out our two pence and give them to the host, without saying, 'When I come again, thou shalt give me fourpence,' there is a capacity of noble passion left in our hearts' core. We show it in our work – in our war, – even in those unjust domestic affections which make us furious at a small private wrong, while we are polite to a boundless public one: we are still industrious to the last hour of the day, though we add the gambler's fury to the labourer's patience; we are still brave to the death, though incapable of discerning true cause for battle; and are still true in affection to our own flesh, to the death, as the sea-monsters are, and the rock-eagles. And there is hope for a nation while this can be still said of it. As long as it holds its life in its hand, ready to give it for its honour (though a foolish honour), for its love (though a selfish love), and for its business (though a base business), there is hope for it. But hope only; for this instinctive, reckless virtue cannot last. No nation can last, which has made a mob of itself, however generous at heart. It must discipline its passions, and direct them, or they will discipline *it*, one day, with scorpion whips. Above all, a nation cannot last as a money-making mob: it cannot with impunity, – it cannot with existence, – go on despising literature, despising science, despising art, despising nature, despising compassion, and concentrating its soul on Pence. Do you think these are harsh or wild words? Have patience with me but a little longer. I will prove their truth to you, clause by clause.

(I.) I say first we have despised literature. What do we, as a nation, care about books? How much do you think we spend altogether on our libraries, public or private, as compared with what we spend on our horses? If a man spends lavishly on his library, you call him mad – a bibliomaniac. But you never call any one a horsemaniac, though men ruin themselves every day by their horses, and you do not hear of people ruining themselves by their books. Or, to go lower still, how much do you think the contents of the book-shelves of the United Kingdom, public and private, would fetch, as compared with the contents of its wine-cellars? What position would its expenditure on literature take, as compared with its expenditure on luxurious eating? We talk of food for the mind, as of food for the body: now a good book contains such food inexhaustibly; it is a provision for life, and for the best part of us; yet how long most people would look at the best book before they would give the price of a large turbot for it? Though there have been men who have pinched their stomachs and bared their backs to buy a book, whose libraries were cheaper to them, I think, in the end, than most men's dinners are. We are few of us put to such trial, and more the pity; for, indeed, a precious thing is all the more precious to us if it has been won by work or economy; and if public libraries were half so costly as public dinners, or books cost the tenth part of what bracelets do, even foolish men and women might sometimes suspect there was good in reading, as well as in munching and sparkling: whereas the very cheapness of literature is making even wise people forget that if a book is worth reading, it is worth buying. No book is worth anything which is not worth *much*; nor is it serviceable, until it has been read, and re-read, and loved, and loved again; and marked, so that you can refer to the passages you want in it, as a soldier can seize the weapon he needs in an armoury, or a housewife bring the spice she needs from her store. Bread of flour is good; but there is bread, sweet as honey, if we would eat it, in a good book; and the family must be poor indeed, which, once in their lives, cannot, for such multipliable barley-loaves, pay their baker's bill. We call ourselves a rich nation, and we are filthy and foolish enough to thumb each other's books out of circulating libraries!

(II.) I say we have despised science. 'What!' you exclaim, 'are we not foremost in all discovery,³ and is not the whole world giddy by reason, or unreason, of our inventions?' Yes; but do you suppose that is national work? That work is all done *in spite* of the nation; by private people's zeal and money. We are glad enough, indeed, to make our profit of science; we snap up anything in the way of a scientific bone that has meat on it, eagerly enough; but if the scientific man comes for a bone or a crust to *us*, that is another story. What have we publicly done for science? We are obliged to know what o'clock it is, for the safety of our ships, and therefore we pay for an observatory; and we allow ourselves, in the person of our Parliament, to be annually tormented into doing something, in a slovenly way, for the British Museum; sullenly apprehending that to be a place for keeping stuffed birds in, to amuse our children. If anybody will pay for their own telescope, and resolve another nebula, we cackle over the discernment as if it were our own; if one in ten thousand of our hunting squires suddenly perceives that the earth was indeed made to be something else than a portion for foxes, and burrows in it himself, and tells us where the gold is, and where the coals, we understand that there is some use in that; and very properly knight him: but is the accident of his having found out how to employ himself usefully any credit to *us*? (The negation of such discovery among his brother squires may perhaps be some *dis*credit to us, if we would consider of it.) But if you doubt these generalities, here is one fact for us all to mediate upon, illustrative of our love of science. Two years ago there was a collection of the fossils of Solenhofen to be sold in Bavaria; the best in existence, containing many specimens unique for perfectness, and one unique as an example of a species (a whole kingdom of unknown living creatures being announced by that fossil). This collection, of which the mere market worth, among private buyers, would probably have been some thousand or twelve hundred pounds, was offered to the English nation for seven hundred: but we would not give seven hundred, and the whole series would have been in the Munich Museum at this moment, if Professor Owen had not, with loss of his own time, and patient tormenting of the British public in person of its representatives, got leave to give four hundred pounds at once, and himself became answerable for the other three! which the said public will doubtless pay him eventually, but sulkily, and caring nothing about the matter all the while; only always ready to cackle if any credit comes of it. Consider, I beg of you, arithmetically, what this fact means. Your annual expenditure for public purposes, (a third of it for military apparatus,) is at least 50 millions. Now £700 is to £50,000,000 roughly, as seven pence to two thousand pounds. Suppose, then, a gentleman of unknown income, but whose wealth was to be conjectured from the fact that he spent two thousand a year on his park-walls and footmen only, professes himself fond of science; and that one of his servants comes eagerly to tell him that an unique collection of fossils, giving clue to a new era of creation, is to be had for a sum of seven pence sterling; and that the gentleman who is fond of science, and spends two thousand a year on his park, answers, after keeping his servant waiting several months, 'Well! I'll give you fourpence for them, if you will be answerable for the extra threepence yourself, till next year!'

(III.) I say you have despised Art! 'What!' you again answer, 'have we not Art exhibitions, miles long? and do we not pay thousands of pounds for single pictures? and have we not Art schools and institutions, more than ever nation had before?' Yes, truly, but all that is for the sake of the shop. You would fain sell canvas as well as coals, and crockery as well as iron; you would take every other nation's bread out of its mouth if you could; not being able to do that, your ideal of life is to stand in the thoroughfares of the world, like Ludgate apprentices, screaming to every passer-by, 'What d'ye lack?' You know nothing of your own faculties or circumstances; you fancy that, among your damp, flat, fat fields of clay, you can have as quick art-fancy as the Frenchman among his bronzed vines, or the Italian under his volcanic cliffs; – that Art may be learned, as book-keeping is, and when learned, will give you more books to keep. You care for pictures, absolutely, no more than you do for the bills pasted on your dead walls. There is always room on the walls for the bills to be read, – never for the pictures to be seen. You do not know what pictures you have (by repute) in the country, nor whether they are false or true, nor whether they are taken care of or not; in foreign countries, you calmly see the noblest existing pictures in the world rotting in abandoned wreck – (in Venice you saw the Austrian guns deliberately pointed at the palaces containing them), and if you heard that all the fine pictures in Europe were made into sand-bags to-morrow on the Austrian forts, it would not trouble you so much as the chance of a brace or two of game less in your own bags, in a day's shooting. That is your national love of Art.

(IV.) You have despised Nature; that is to say, all the deep and sacred sensations of natural scenery. The French revolutionists made stables of the cathedrals of France; you have made race-courses of the cathedrals of the earth. Your *one* conception of pleasure is to drive in railroad carriages round their aisles, and eat off their altars.[4] You have put a railroad-bridge over the falls of Schaffhausen. You have tunnelled the cliffs of Lucerne by Tell's chapel; you have destroyed the Clarens shore of the Lake of Geneva; there is not a quiet valley in England that you have not filled with bellowing fire; there is no particle left of English land which you have not trampled coal ashes into[5] – nor any foreign city in which the spread of your presence is not marked among its fair old streets and happy gardens by a consuming white leprosy of new hotels and perfumers' shops: the Alps themselves, which your own poets used to love so reverently, you look upon as soaped poles in a bear-garden, which you set yourselves to climb and slide down again, with 'shrieks of delight.' When you are past shrieking, having no human articulate voice to say you are glad with, you fill the quietude of their valleys with gunpowder blasts, and rush home, red with cutaneous eruption of conceit, and voluble with convulsive hiccough of self-satisfaction. I think nearly the two sorrowfullest spectacles I have ever seen in humanity, taking the deep inner significance of them, are the English mobs in the valley of Chamouni, amusing themselves with firing rusty howitzers; and the Swiss vintagers of Zurich expressing their Christian thanks for the gift of the vine, by assembling in knots in the 'towers of the vineyards,' and slowly loading and firing horse-pistols from morning till evening. It is pitiful, to have dim conceptions of duty; more pitiful, it seems to me, to have conceptions like these, of mirth.

Lastly. You despise compassion. There is no need of words of mine for proof of this. I will merely print one of the newspaper paragraphs which I am in the habit of cutting out and throwing into my store-drawer; here is one from a *Morning Post* of an early date this year (1865); [. . .] it relates only one of such facts as happen now daily; this by chance having taken a form in which it came before the coroner. I will print the paragraph in red. Be sure, the facts themselves are written in that colour, in a book which we shall all of us, literate or illiterate, have to read our page of, some day.

'An inquiry was held on Friday by Mr Richards, deputy coroner, at the White Horse Tavern, Christ Church, Spitalfields, respecting the death of Michael Collins, aged 58 years. Mary Collins, a miserable-looking woman, said that she lived with the deceased and his son in a room at 2, Cobb's Court, Christ Church. Deceased was a "translator" of boots. Witness went out and bought old boots; deceased and his son made them into good ones, and then witness sold them for what she could get at the shops, which was very little indeed. Deceased and his son used to work night and day to try and get a little bread and tea, and pay for the room (2s. a week), so as to keep the home together. On Friday-night-week deceased got up from his bench and began to shiver. He threw down the boots, saying, "Somebody else must finish them when I am gone, for I can do no more." There was no fire, and he said, "I would be better if I was warm." Witness therefore took two pairs of translated boots to sell at the shop, but she could only get 14d. for the two pairs, for the people at the shop said, "We must have our profit." Witness got 14 lb. of coal, and a little tea and bread. Her son sat up the whole night to make the "translations," to get money, but deceased died on Saturday morning. The family never had enough to eat. – Coroner: "It seems to me deplorable that you did not go into the workhouse." Witness: "We wanted the comforts of our little home." A juror asked what the comforts were, for he only saw a little straw in the corner of the room, the windows of which were broken. The witness began to cry, and said that they had a quilt and other little things. The deceased said he never would go into the workhouse. In summer, when the season was good, they sometimes made as much as 10s. profit in the week. They then always saved towards the next week, which was generally a bad one. In winter they made not half so much. For three years they had been getting from bad to worse. – Cornelius Collins said that he had assisted his father since 1847. They used to work so far into the night that both nearly lost their eyesight. Witness now had a film over his eyes. Five years ago deceased applied to the parish for aid. The relieving officer gave him a 4 lb. loaf, and told him if he came again he should "get the stones."[6] That disgusted deceased, and he would have nothing to do with them since. They got worse and worse until last Friday week, when they had not even a halfpenny to buy a candle. Deceased then lay down on the straw, and said he could not live till morning. – A juror: "You are dying of starvation yourself, and you ought to go into the house until the summer." – Witness: "If we went in we should die. When we come out in the summer we should be like people dropped from the sky. No one would know us, and we would not have even a room. I could work now if I had food, for my sight would get better.' Dr G. P. Walker said deceased died from syncope, from exhaustion from want of food. The deceased had had no bedclothes. For four months he had had nothing but bread to eat. There was not a particle of fat in the body. There was no disease, but, if there had been medical attendance, he might have survived the syncope or fainting. The Coroner having remarked upon the painful nature of the case, the jury returned the following verdict: "That deceased died from exhaustion from want of food and the common necessaries of life; also through want of medical aid."'

'Why would witness not go into the workhouse?' you ask. Well, the poor seem to have a prejudice against the workhouse which the rich have not; for of course everyone who takes a pension from Government goes into the workhouse on a grand scale:[7] only the work-houses for the rich do not involve the idea of work, and should be called play-houses. But the poor like to die independently, it appears; perhaps if we made the play-houses for them pretty and pleasant enough, or gave them their pensions at home, and allowed them a little introductory peculation with the public money, their minds might be reconciled to the conditions. Meantime, here are the facts: we make our relief either so insulting to them, or so painful, that they rather die than take it at our hands; or, for third alternative, we leave them so untaught and foolish that they starve like brute creatures, wild and dumb, not knowing what to do, or what to ask. I say, you despise compassion; if you did not, such a newspaper paragraph would be as impossible in a Christian country as a deliberate assassination permitted in its public streets. 'Christian,' did I say? Alas! if we were but wholesomely *un*-Christian, it would be impossible: it is our imaginary Christianity that helps us to commit these crimes, for we revel and luxuriate in our faith, for the lewd sensation of it; dressing *it* up, like everything else, in fiction. The dramatic Christianity of the organ and aisle, of dawn-service and twilight-revival – the Christianity, which we do not fear to mix the mockery of, pictorially, with our play about the devil, in our Satanellas, – Roberts, – Fausts; chanting hymns through traceried windows for background effect, and artistically modulating the 'Dio' through variation on variation of mimicked prayer: (while we distribute tracts, next day, for the benefit of uncultivated swearers, upon what we suppose to be the signification of the Third Commandment; –) this gas-lighted, and gas-inspired Christianity, we are triumphant in, and draw back the hem of our robes from the touch of the heretics who dispute it. But to do a piece of common Christian righteousness in a plain English word or deed; to make Christian law any rule of life, and found one National act or hope thereon, – we know too well what our faith comes to for that! You might sooner get lightning out of incense smoke than true action or passion out of your modern English religion. You had better get rid of the smoke, and the organ pipes, both: leave them, and the Gothic windows, and the painted glass, to the property man; give up your carburetted hydrogen ghost in one healthy expiration, and look after Lazarus at the doorstep. For there is a true Church wherever one hand meets another helpfully, and that is the only holy or Mother Church which ever was, or ever shall be.

All these pleasures then, and all these virtues, I repeat, you nationally despise. You have, indeed, men among you who do not; by whose work, by whose strength, by whose life, by whose death, you live, and never thank them. Your wealth, your amusement, your pride, would all be alike impossible, but for those whom you scorn or forget. The policeman, who is walking up and down the black lane all night to watch the guilt you have created there; and may have his brains beaten out, and be maimed for life, at any moment, and never be thanked; the sailor wrestling with the sea's rage; the quiet student poring over his book or his vial; the common worker, without praise, and nearly without bread, fulfilling his task as your horses drag your carts, hopeless, and spurned of all: these are the men by whom England lives; but they are not the nation; they are only the body and nervous force of it, acting still from old habit in a convulsive perseverance, while the mind is gone. Our National wish and purpose are only to be amused; our National religion is the performance of church ceremonies, and preaching of soporific truths (or untruths) to keep the mob quietly at work, while we amuse ourselves; and the necessity for this amusement is fastening on us, as a feverous disease of parched throat and wandering eyes – senseless, dissolute, merciless. How literally that word *Dis*-Ease, the Negation and impossibility of Ease, expressed the entire moral state of our English Industry and its Amusements!

When men are rightly occupied, their amusement grows out of their work, as the colour-petals out of a fruitful flower; – when they are faithfully helpful and compassionate, all their emotions become steady, deep, perpetual, and vivifying to the soul as the natural pulse to the body. But now, having no true business, we pour our whole masculine energy into the false business of money-making; and having no true emotion, we must have false emotions dressed up for us to play with, not innocently, as children with dolls, but guiltily and darkly, as the idolatrous Jews with their pictures on cavern walls, which men had to dig to detect. The justice we do not execute, we mimic in the novel and on the stage; for the beauty we destroy in nature, we substitute the metamor-phosis of the pantomime, and (the human nature of us imperatively requiring awe and sorrow of *some* kind) for the noble grief we should have borne with our fellows, and the pure tears we should have wept with them, we gloat over the pathos of the police court, and gather the night-dew of the grave.

It is difficult to estimate the true significance of these things; the facts are frightful enough; – the measure of national fault involved in them is perhaps not as great as it would at first seem. We permit, or cause, thousands of deaths daily, but we mean no harm; we set fire to houses, and ravage peasants' fields, yet we should be sorry to find we had injured anybody. We are still kind at heart; still capable of virtue, but only as children are. Chalmers, at the end of his long life, having had much power with the public, being plagued in some serious matter by a reference to 'public opinion,' uttered the impatient exclamation, 'The public is just a great baby!' And the reason that I have allowed all these graver subjects of thought to mix themselves up with an inquiry into methods of reading, is that, the more I see of our national faults or miseries, the more they resolve themselves into conditions of childish illiterateness and want of education in the most ordinary habits of thought. It is, I repeat, not vice, not selfishness, not dulness of brain, which we have to lament; but an un-reachable schoolboy's recklessness, only differing from the true schoolboy's in its incapacity of being helped, because it acknowledges no master.

There is a curious type of us given in one of the lovely, neglected works of the last of our great painters. It is a drawing of Kirkby Lonsdale churchyard, and of its brook, and valley, and hills, and folded morning sky beyond. And unmindful alike of these, and of the dead who have left these for other valleys and for other skies, a group of schoolboys have piled their little books upon a grave, to strike them off with stones. So, also, we play with the words of the dead that would teach us, and strike them far from us with our bitter, reckless will; little thinking that those leaves which the wind scatters had been piled, not only upon a gravestone, but upon the seal of an enchanted vault – nay, the gate of a great city of sleeping kings, who would awake for us and walk with us, if we knew but how to call them by their names. How often, even if we lift the marble entrance gate, do we but wander among those old kings in their repose, and finger the robes they lie in, and stir the crowns on their foreheads; and still they are silent to us, and seem but a dusty imagery; because we know not the incantation of the heart that would wake them; – which, if they once heard, they would start up to meet us in their power of long ago, narrowly to look upon us, and consider us; and, as the fallen kings of Hades meet the newly fallen, saying, 'Art thou also become weak as we – art thou also become one of us?' so would these kings, with their undimmed, unshaken diadems, meet us, saying, 'Art thou also become pure and mighty of heart as we – art thou also become one of us?'

Mighty of heart, mighty of mind – 'magnanimous' – to be this, is indeed to be great in life; to become this increasingly, is, indeed, to 'advance in life,' – in life itself – not in the trappings of it. My friends, do you remember that old Scythian custom, when the head of a house died? How he was dressed in his finest dress, and set in his chariot, and carried about to his friends' houses; and each of them placed him at his table's head, and all feasted in his presence? Suppose it were offered to you in plain words, as it *is* offered to you in dire facts, that you should gain this Scythian honour, gradually, while you yet thought yourself alive. Suppose the offer were this: You shall die slowly; your blood shall daily grow cold, your flesh petrify, your heart beat at last only as a rusted group of iron valves. Your life shall fade from you, and sink through the earth into the ice of Caina; but, day by day, your body shall be dressed more gaily, and set in higher chariots, and have more orders on its breast – crowns on its head, if you will. Men shall bow before it, stare and shout round it, crowd after it up and down the streets; build palaces for it, feast with it at their tables' heads all the night long; your soul shall stay enough within it to know what they do, and feel the weight of the golden dress on its shoulders, and the furrow of the crown-edge on the skull; – no more. Would you take the offer, verbally made by the death-angel? Would the meanest among us take it, think you? Yet practically and verily we grasp at it, every one of us, in a measure; many of us grasp at it in its fulness of horror. Every man accepts it, who desires to advance in life without knowing what life is; who means only that he is to get more horses, and more footmen, and more fortune, and more public honour, and – *not* more personal soul. He only is advancing in life, whose heart is getting softer, whose blood warmer, whose brain quicker, whose spirit is entering into Living peace. And the men who have this life in them are the true lords or kings of the earth – they, and they only. All other kingships, so far as they are true, are only the practical issue and expression of theirs; if less than this, they are either dramatic royalties, – costly shows, set off, indeed, with real jewels, instead of tinsel – but still only the toys of nations; or else they are no royalties at all, but tyrannies, or the mere active and practical issue of national folly;

for which reason I have said of them elsewhere, 'Visible governments are the toys of some nations, the diseases of others, the harness of some, the burdens of more.'

But I have no words for the wonder with which I hear Kinghood still spoken of, even among thoughtful men, as if governed nations were a personal property, and might be bought and sold, or otherwise acquired, as sheep, of whose flesh their king was to feed, and whose fleece he was to gather; as if Achilles' indignant epithet of base kings, 'people-eating,' were the constant and proper title of all monarchs; and the enlargement of a king's dominion meant the same thing as the increase of a private man's estate! Kings who think so, however powerful, can no more be the true kings of the nation than gadflies are the kings of a horse; they suck it, and may drive it wild, but do not guide it. They, and their courts, and their armies are, if one could see clearly, only a large species of marsh mosquito, with bayonet proboscis and melodious, band-mastered trumpeting, in the summer air; the twilight being, perhaps, sometimes fairer, but hardly more wholesome, for its glittering mists of midge companies. The true kings, meanwhile, rule quietly, if at all, and hate ruling; too many of them make 'il gran rifiuto'; and if they do not, the mob, as soon as they are likely to become useful to it, is pretty sure to make *its* 'gran rifiuto' of *them*.

Yet the visible king may also be a true one, some day, if ever day comes when he will estimate his dominion by the *force* of it, – not the geographical boundaries. It matters very little whether Trent cuts you a cantel out here, or Rhine rounds you a castle less there. But it does matter to you, king of men, whether you can verily say to this man, 'Go,' and he goeth; and to another, 'Come,' and he cometh. Whether you can turn your people, as you can Trent – and where it is that you bid them come, and where go. It matters to you, king of men, whether your people hate you, and die by you, or love you, and live by you. You may measure your dominion by multitudes, better than by miles; and count degrees of love-latitude, not from, but to, a wonderfully warm and infinite equator.

Measure! – nay, you cannot measure. Who shall measure the difference between the power of those who 'do and teach,' and who are greatest in the kingdoms of earth, as of heaven – and the power of those who undo, and consume – whose power, at the fullest, is only the power of the moth and the rust? Strange! to think how the Moth-kings lay up treasures for the moth; and the Rust-kings, who are to their peoples' strength as rust to armour, lay up treasures for the rust; and the Robber-kings, treasures for the robber; but how few kings have ever laid up treasures that needed no guarding – treasures of which, the more thieves there were, the better! Broidered robe, only to be rent; helm and sword, only to be dimmed; jewel and gold, only to be scattered; – there have been three kinds of kings who have gathered these. Suppose there ever should arise a Fourth order of kings, who had read, in some obscure writing of long ago, that there was a Fourth kind of treasure, which the jewel and gold could not equal, neither should it be valued with pure gold. A web made fair in the weaving, by Athena's shuttle; an armour, forged in divine fire by Vulcanian force; a gold to be mined in the very sun's red heart, where he sets over the Delphian cliffs; – deep-pictured tissue; – impenetrable armour; – potable gold! – the three great Angels of Conduct, Toil, and Thought, still calling to us, and waiting at the posts of our doors, to lead us, with their winged power, and guide us, with their unerring eyes, by the path which no fowl knoweth, and which the vulture's eye has not seen! Suppose kings should ever arise, who heard and believed this word, and at last gathered and brought forth treasures of – Wisdom – for their people?

Think what an amazing business *that* would be! How inconceivable, in the state of our present national wisdom! That we should bring up our peasants to a book exercise instead of a bayonet exercise! – organise, drill, maintain with pay, and good generalship, armies of thinkers, instead of armies of stabbers! – find national amusement in reading-rooms as well as rifle-grounds; give prizes for a fair shot at a fact, as well as for a leaden splash on a target. What an absurd idea it seems, put fairly in words, that the wealth of the capitalists of civilized nations should ever come to support literature instead of war!

Have yet patience with me, while I read you a single sentence out of the only book, properly to be called a book, that I have yet written myself, the one that will stand (if anything stand), surest and longest of all work of mine.

'It is one very awful form of the operation of wealth in Europe that it is entirely capitalists' wealth which supports unjust wars. Just wars do not need so much money to support them;

for most of the men who wage such, wage them gratis; but for an unjust war, men's bodies and souls have both to be bought; and the best tools of war for them besides, which make such war costly to the maximum; not to speak of the cost of base fear, and angry suspicion, between nations which have not grace nor honesty enough in all their multitudes to buy an hour's peace of mind with; as, at present, France and England, purchasing of each other ten millions sterling worth of consternation, annually (a remarkably light crop, half thorns and half aspen leaves, sown, reaped, and granaried by the "science" of the modern political economist, teaching covetousness instead of truth). And, all unjust war being supportable, if not by pillage of the enemy, only by loans from capitalists, these loans are repaid by subsequent taxation of the people, who appear to have no will in the matter, the capitalists' will being the primary root of the war; but its real root is the covetousness of the whole nation, rendering it incapable of faith, frankness, or justice, and bringing about, therefore, in due time, his own separate loss and punishment to each person.'

France and England literally, observe, buy *panic* of each other; they pay, each of them, for ten thousand-thousand-pounds'-worth of terror, a year. Now suppose, instead of buying these ten millions' worth of panic annually, they made up their minds to be at peace with each other, and buy ten millions' worth of knowledge annually; and that each nation spent its ten thousand thousand pounds a year in founding royal libraries, royal art galleries, royal museums, royal gardens, and places of rest. Might it not be better somewhat for both French and English?

It will be long, yet, before that comes to pass. Nevertheless, I hope it will not be long before royal or national libraries will be founded in every considerable city, with a royal series of books in them; the same series in every one of them, chosen books, the best in every kind, prepared for that national series in the most perfect way possible; their text printed all on leaves of equal size, broad of margin, and divided into pleasant volumes, light in the hand, beautiful, and strong, and thorough as examples of binders' work; and that these great libraries will be accessible to all clean and orderly persons at all times of the day and evening; strict law being enforced for this cleanliness and quietness.

I could shape for you other plans, for art-galleries, and for natural history galleries, and for many precious – many, it seems to me, needful – things; but this book plan is the easiest and needfullest, and would prove a considerable tonic to what we call our British constitution, which has fallen dropsical of late, and has an evil thirst, and evil hunger, and wants healthier feeding. You have got its corn laws repealed for it; try if you cannot get corn laws established for it, dealing in a better bread; – bread made of that old enchanted Arabian grain, the Sesame, which opens doors; – doors not of robbers', but of Kings' Treasuries.

Notes

1. 2 Peter iii. 5–7.
2. Modern 'Education' for the most part signifies giving
    people the faculty of thinking wrong on every conceivable
    subject of importance to them.
3. Since this was written, the answer has become definitely
    – No; we having surrendered the field of Arctic discovery
    to the Continental nations, as being ourselves too poor
    to pay for ships.
4. I meant that the beautiful places of the world – Switzer-
    land, Italy, South Germany, and so on – are, indeed, the
    truest cathedrals – places to be reverent in, and to worship
    in; and that we only care to drive through them: and to
    eat and drink at their most sacred places.
5. I was singularly struck, some years ago, by finding all the
    river shore at Richmond, in Yorkshire, black in its earth,
    from the mere drift of soot-laden air from places many
    miles away.
6. This abbreviation of the penalty of useless labour is curi-
    ously coincident in verbal form with a certain passage
    which some of us may remember. It may perhaps be well
    to preserve beside this paragraph another cutting out of
    my store-drawer, from the *Morning Post*, of about a parallel
    date, Friday, March 10th, 1865: – 'The *salons* of Mme. C –,
    who did the honours with clever imitative grace and
    elegance, were crowded with princes, dukes, marquises,
    and counts – in fact, with the same *male* company as
    one meets at the parties of the Princess Metternich and
    Madame Drouyn de Lhuys. Some English peers and
    members of Parliament were present, and appeared to
    enjoy the animated and dazzlingly improper scene. On
    the second floor the supper tables were loaded with every

delicacy of the season. That your readers may form some idea of the dainty fare of the Parisian demi-monde, I copy the menu of the supper, which was served to all the guests (about 200) seated at four o'clock. Choice Yquem, Johannisberg, Laffitte, Tokay, and champagne of the finest vintages were served most lavishly throughout the morning. After supper dancing was resumed with increased animation, and the ball terminated with a *chaîne diabolique* and a *cancan d'enfer* at seven in the morning. (Morning service – 'Ere the fresh lawns appeared, under the opening eyelids of the Morn. – ') Here is the menu: – "Consommé de volaille à la Bagration: 16 hors-d'œuvres variés. Bouchées à la Talleyrand. Saumons froids, sauce Ravigote. Filets de bœuf en Bellevue, timbales milanaises, chaudfroid de gibier. Dindes truffées. Pâtés de foies gras, buissons d'écrevisses, salades vénétiennes, gelées blanches aux fruits, gâteaux mancini, parisiens et parisiennes. Fromages glacés. Ananas. Dessert." '

7. Please observe this statement, and think of it, and consider how it happens that a poor old woman will be ashamed to take a shilling a week from the country – but no one is ashamed to take a pension of a thousand a year.

Traffic

Delivered in the Town Hall, Bradford
[April 21, 1864]

My good Yorkshire friends, you asked me down here among your hills that I might talk to you about this Exchange you are going to build: but, earnestly and seriously asking you to pardon me, I am going to do nothing of the kind. I cannot talk, or at least can say very little, about this same Exchange. I must talk of quite other things, though not willingly; – I could not deserve your pardon, if, when you invited me to speak on one subject, I *wilfully* spoke on another. But I cannot speak, to purpose, of anything about which I do not care; and most simply and sorrowfully I have to tell you, in the outset, that I do *not* care about this Exchange of yours.

If, however, when you sent me your invitation, I had answered, 'I won't come, I don't care about the Exchange of Bradford,' you would have been justly offended with me, not knowing the reasons of so blunt a carelessness. So I have come down, hoping that you will patiently let me tell you why, on this, and many other such occasions, I now remain silent, when formerly I should have caught at the opportunity of speaking to a gracious audience.

In a word, then, I do not care about this Exchange – because *you* don't; and because you know perfectly well

I cannot make you. Look at the essential conditions of the case, which you, as business men, know perfectly well, though perhaps you think I forget them. You are going to spend £30,000, which to you, collectively, is nothing; the buying a new coat is, as to the cost of it, a much more important matter of consideration to me, than building a new Exchange is to you. But you think you may as well have the right thing for your money. You know there are a great many odd styles of architecture about; you don't want to do anything ridiculous; you hear of me, among others, as a respectable architectural man-milliner; and you send for me, that I may tell you the leading fashion; and what is, in our shops, for the moment, the newest and sweetest thing in pinnacles.

Now, pardon me for telling you frankly, you cannot have good architecture merely by asking people's advice on occasion. All good architecture is the expression of national life and character; and it is produced by a prevalent and eager national taste, or desire for beauty. And I want you to think a little of the deep significance of this word 'taste'; for no statement of mine has been more earnestly or oftener controverted than that good taste is essentially a moral quality. 'No,' say many of my antagonists, 'taste is one thing, morality is another. Tell us what is pretty: we shall be glad to know that; but we need no sermons – even were you able to preach them, which may be doubted.'

Permit me, therefore, to fortify this old dogma of mine somewhat. Taste is not only a part and an index of morality; – it is the ONLY morality. The first, and last, and closest trial question to any living creature is, 'What do you like?' Tell me what you like, and I'll tell you what you are. Go out into the street, and ask the first man or woman you meet, what their 'taste' is; and if they answer candidly, you know them, body and soul. 'You, my friend in the rags, with the unsteady gait, what do *you* like?' 'A pipe, and a quartern of gin.' I know you. 'You, good woman, with the quick step and tidy bonnet, what do you like?' 'A swept hearth, and a clean tea-table; and my husband opposite me, and a baby at my breast.' Good, I know you also. 'You, little girl with the golden hair and the soft eyes, what do you like?' 'My canary, and a run among the wood hyacinths.' 'You, little boy with the dirty hands, and the low forehead, what do you like?' 'A shy at the sparrows, and a game at pitch farthing.' Good; we know them all now. What more need we ask?

'Nay,' perhaps you answer; 'we need rather to ask what these people and children do, than what they like. If they *do* right, it is no matter that they like what is wrong; and if they *do* wrong, it is no matter that they like what is right. Doing is the great thing; and it does not matter that the man likes drinking, so that he does not drink; nor that the little girl likes to be kind to her canary, if she will not learn her lessons; nor that the little boy likes throwing stones at the sparrows, if he goes to the Sunday school.' Indeed, for a short time, and in a provisional sense, this is true. For if, resolutely, people do what is right, in time to come they like doing it. But they only are in a right moral state when they *have* come to like doing it; and as long as they don't like it, they are still in a vicious state. The man is not in health of body who is always thinking of the bottle in the cupboard, though he bravely bears his thirst; but the man who heartily enjoys water in the morning, and wine in the evening, each in its proper quantity and time. And the entire object of true education is to make people not merely *do* the right things, but *enjoy* the right things: – not merely industrious, but to love industry – not merely learned, but to love knowledge – not merely pure, but to love purity – not merely just, but to hunger and thirst after justice.

But you may answer or think, 'Is the liking for outside ornaments, – for pictures, or statues, or furniture, or architecture, a moral quality?' Yes, most surely, if a rightly set liking. Taste for *any* pictures or statues is not a moral quality, but taste for good ones is. Only here again we have to define the word 'good.' I don't mean by 'good,' clever – or learned – or difficult in the doing. Take a picture by Teniers, of sots quarrelling over their dice; it is an entirely clever picture; so clever that nothing in its kind has ever been done equal to it; but it is also an entirely base and evil picture. It is an expression of delight in the prolonged contemplation of a vile thing, and delight in that is an 'unmannered,' or 'immoral' quality. It is 'bad taste' in the profoundest sense – it is the taste of the devils. On the other hand, a picture of Titian's, or a Greek statue, or a Greek coin, or a Turner landscape, expresses delight in the perpetual contemplation of a good and perfect thing. That is an entirely moral quality – it is the taste of the angels. And all delight in fine art, and all love of it, resolve themselves into simple love of that which deserves love. That deserving is the quality which we call 'loveliness' – (we ought to have an opposite word, hateliness, to be said of the things which deserve to be hated); and it is not an indifferent nor optional thing whether we love this or that; but it is just the vital function of all our being. What we *like* determines what we *are*, and is the sign of what we are; and to teach taste is inevitably to form character.

As I was thinking over this, in walking up Fleet Street the other day, my eye caught the title of a book standing open in a bookseller's window. It was – *On the necessity of the diffusion of taste among all classes.* 'Ah,' I thought to myself, 'my classifying friend, when you have diffused your taste, where will your classes be? The man who likes what you like, belongs to the same class with you, I think. Inevitably so. You may put him to other work if you choose; but, by the condition you have brought him into, he will dislike the work as much as you would your-self. You get hold of a scavenger or a costermonger, who enjoyed the Newgate Calendar for literature, and "Pop goes the Weasel" for music. You think you can make him like Dante and Beethoven? I wish you joy of your lessons; but if you do, you have made a gentleman of him: – he won't like to go back to his costermongering.'

And so completely and unexceptionally is this so, that, if I had time to-night, I could show you that a nation cannot be affected by any vice, or weakness, without expressing it, legibly, and for ever, either in bad art, or by want of art; and that there is no national virtue, small or great, which is not manifestly expressed in all the art which circumstances enable the people possessing that virtue to produce. Take, for instance, your great English virtue of enduring and patient courage. You have at present in England only one art of any consequence – that is, iron-working. You know thoroughly well how to cast and hammer iron. Now, do you think, in those masses of lava which you build volcanic cones to melt, and which you forge at the mouths of the Infernos you have created; do you think, on those iron plates, your courage and endurance are not written for ever, – not merely with an iron pen, but on iron parchment? And take also your great English vice – European vice – vice of all the world – vice of all other worlds that roll or shine in heaven, bearing with them yet the atmosphere of hell – the vice of jealousy, which brings competition into your commerce, treachery into your councils, and dishonour into your wars – that vice which has rendered for you, and for your next neighbouring nation, the daily occupations of existence no longer possible, but with the mail upon your breasts and the sword loose in its sheath; so that at last, you have realized for all the multitudes of the two great peoples who lead the so-called civilization of the earth, – you have realized for them all, I say, in person and in policy, what was once true only of the rough Border riders of your Cheviot hills –

> 'They carved at the meal
> With gloves of steel,
> And they drank the red wine through the helmet barr'd;' –

do you think that this national shame and dastardliness of heart are not written as legibly on every rivet of your iron armour as the strength of the right hands that forged it?

Friends, I know not whether this thing be the more ludicrous or the more melancholy. It is quite unspeakably both. Suppose, instead of being now sent for by you, I had been sent for by some private gentleman, living in a suburban house, with his garden separated only by a fruit wall from his next door neighbour's; and he had called me to consult with him on the furnishing of his drawing-room. I begin looking about me, and find the walls rather bare; I think such and such a paper might be desirable – perhaps a little fresco here and there on the ceiling – a damask curtain or so at the windows. 'Ah,' says my employer, 'damask curtains, indeed! That's all very fine, but you know I can't afford that kind of thing just now!' 'Yet the world credits you with a splendid income!' 'Ah, yes,' says my friend, 'but do you know, at present I am obliged to spend it nearly all in steel-traps?' 'Steel-traps! for whom?' 'Why, for that fellow on the other side the wall, you know: we're very good friends, capital friends; but we are obliged to keep our traps set on both sides of the wall; we could not possibly keep on friendly terms without them, and our spring guns. The worst of it is, we are both clever fellows enough; and there's never a day passes that we don't find out a new trap, or a new gun-barrel, or something; we spend about fifteen millions a year each in our traps, take it altogether; and I don't see how we're to do with less.' A highly comic state of life for two private gentlemen! but for two nations, it seems to me, not wholly comic. Bedlam would be comic, perhaps, if there were only one mad-man in it; and your Christmas pantomime is comic, when there is only one clown in it; but when the whole world turns clown, and paints itself red with its own heart's blood instead of vermilion, it is something else than comic, I think.

Mind, I know a great deal of this is play, and willingly allow for that. You don't know what to do with yourselves for a sensation: fox-hunting and cricketing will not carry you through the whole of this unendurably long mortal life: you liked pop-guns when you were schoolboys, and rifles and Armstrongs are only the same things better made: but then the worst of it is, that what was play to you when boys, was not play to the sparrows; and what is play to you now, is not play to the small birds of State neither; and for the black eagles, you are somewhat shy of taking shots at them, if I mistake not.

I must get back to the matter in hand, however. Believe me, without farther instance, I could show you, in all time, that every nation's vice, or virtue, was written in its art: the soldiership of early Greece; the sensuality of late Italy; the visionary religion of Tuscany; the splendid human energy of Venice. I have no time to do this to-night (I have done it elsewhere before now); but I proceed to apply the principle to ourselves in a more searching manner.

I notice that among all the new buildings which cover your once wild hills, churches and schools are mixed in due, that is to say, in large proportion, with your mills and mansions; and I notice also that the churches and schools are almost always Gothic, and the mansions and mills are never Gothic. May I ask the meaning of this? for, remember, it is peculiarly a modern phenomenon. When Gothic was invented, houses were Gothic as well as churches; and when the Italian style superseded the Gothic, churches were Italian as well as houses. If there is a Gothic spire to the cathedral of Antwerp, there is a Gothic belfry to the Hôtel de Ville at Brussels; if Inigo Jones builds an Italian Whitehall, Sir Christopher Wren builds an Italian St Paul's. But now you live under one school of architecture, and worship under another. What do you mean by doing this? Am I to understand that you are thinking of changing your architecture back to Gothic; and that you treat your churches experimentally, because it does not matter what mistakes you make in a church? Or am I to understand that you consider Gothic a pre-eminently sacred and beautiful mode of building, which you think, like the fine frankincense, should be mixed for the tabernacle only, and reserved for your religious services? For if this be the feeling, though it may seem at first as if it were graceful and reverent, at the root of the matter, it signifies neither more nor less than that you have separated your religion from your life.

For consider what a wide significance this fact has; and remember that it is not you only, but all the people of England, who are behaving thus, just now.

You have all got into the habit of calling the church 'the house of God.' I have seen, over the doors of many churches, the legend actually carved, '*This* is the house of God and this is the gate of heaven.' Now, note where that legend comes from, and of what place it was first spoken. A boy leaves his father's house to go on a long journey on foot, to visit his uncle: he has to cross a wild hill-desert; just as if one of your own boys had to cross the wolds to visit an uncle at Carlisle. The second or third day your boy finds himself somewhere between Hawes and Brough, in the midst of the moors, at sunset. It is stony ground, and boggy; he cannot go one foot farther that night. Down he lies, to sleep, on Wharnside, where best he may, gathering a few of the stones together to put under his head; – so wild the place is, he cannot get anything but stones. And there, lying under the broad night, he has a dream; and he sees a ladder set up on the earth, and the top of it reaches to heaven, and the angels of God are seen ascending and descending upon it. And when he wakes out of his sleep, he says, 'How dreadful is this place; surely this is none other than the house of God, and this is the gate of heaven.' This PLACE, observe; not this church; not this city; not this stone, even, which he puts up for a memorial – the piece of flint on which his head was lain. But this *place*; this windy slope of Wharnside; this moorland hollow, torrent-bitten, snow-blighted! this *any* place where God lets down the ladder. And how are you to know where that will be? or how are you to determine where it may be, but by being ready for it always? Do you know where the lightning is to fall next? You *do* know that, partly; you can guide the lightning; but you cannot guide the going forth of the Spirit, which is as that lightning when it shines from the east to the west.

But the perpetual and insolent warping of that strong verse to serve a merely ecclesiastical purpose, is only one of the thousand instances in which we sink back into gross Judaism. We call our churches 'temples.' Now, you know perfectly well they are *not* temples. They have never had, never can have, anything whatever to do with temples. They are 'synagogues' – 'gathering places' – where you gather yourselves together as an assembly; and by not calling them so, you again miss the force of another mighty text – 'Thou, when thou prayest, shalt not be as the hypocrites are; for they love to pray standing in the *churches*' [we should translate it], 'that they may be seen of men. But thou, when thou prayest, enter into thy closet, and when thou hast shut thy door, pray to thy Father,' – which is, not in chancel nor in aisle, but 'in secret.'

Now, you feel, as I say this to you – I know you feel – as if I were trying to take away the honour of your churches. Not so; I am trying to prove to you the honour of your houses and your hills; not that the Church is not sacred – but that the whole Earth is. I would have you feel what careless, what constant, what infectious sin there is in all modes of thought, whereby, in calling your churches only 'holy,' you call your hearths and homes 'profane'; and have separated yourselves from the heathen by casting all your household gods to the ground, instead of recognizing, in the places of their many and feeble Lares, the presence of your One and Mighty Lord and Lar.

'But what has all this to do with our Exchange?' you ask me, impatiently. My dear friends, it has just everything to do with it; on these inner and great questions depend all the outer and little ones; and if you have asked me down here to speak to you, because you had before been interested in anything I have written, you must know that all I have yet said about architecture was to show this. The book I called *The Seven Lamps* was to show that certain right states of temper and moral feeling were the magic powers by which all good architecture, without exception, had been produced. *The Stones of Venice* had, from beginning to end, no other aim than to show that the Gothic architecture of Venice had arisen out of, and indicated in all its features, a state of pure national faith, and of domestic virtue; and that its Renaissance architecture had arisen out of, and in all its features indicated, a state of concealed national infidelity, and of domestic corruption. And now, you ask me what style is best to build in, and how can I answer, knowing the meaning of the two styles, but by another question – do you mean to build as Christians or as infidels? And still more – do you mean to build as honest Christians or as honest Infidels? as thoroughly and confessedly either one or the other? You don't like to be asked such rude questions. I cannot help it; they are of much more importance than this Exchange business; and if they can be at once answered, the Exchange business settles itself in a moment. But before I press them farther, I must ask leave to explain one point clearly.

In all my past work, my endeavour has been to show that good architecture is essentially religious – the production of a faithful and virtuous, not of an infidel and corrupted people. But in the course of doing this, I have had also to show that good architecture is not *ecclesiastical*. People are so apt to look upon religion as the business of the clergy, not their own, that the moment they hear of anything depending on 'religion,' they think it must also have depended on the priesthood;

and I have had to take what place was to be occupied between these two errors, and fight both, often with seeming contradiction. Good architecture is the work of good and believing men; therefore, you say, at least some people say, 'Good architecture must essentially have been the work of the clergy, not of the laity.' No – a thousand times no; good architecture has always been the work of the commonalty, *not* of the clergy. 'What,' you say, 'those glorious cathedrals – the pride of Europe – did their builders not form Gothic architecture?' No; they corrupted Gothic architecture. Gothic was formed in the baron's castle, and the burgher's street. It was formed by the thoughts, and hands, and powers of labouring citizens and warrior kings. By the monk it was used as an instrument for the aid of his superstition: when that superstition became a beautiful madness, and the best hearts of Europe vainly dreamed and pined in the cloister, and vainly raged and perished in the crusade, – through that fury of perverted faith and wasted war, the Gothic rose also to its loveliest, most fantastic, and, finally, most foolish dreams; and in those dreams was lost.

I hope, now, that there is no risk of your misunderstanding me when I come to the gist of what I want to say to-night; – when I repeat, that every great national architecture has been the result and exponent of a great national religion. You can't have bits of it here, bits there – you must have it everywhere or nowhere. It is not the monopoly of a clerical company – it is not the exponent of a theological dogma – it is not the hieroglyphic writing of an initiated priesthood; it is the manly language of a people inspired by resolute and common purpose, and rendering resolute and common fidelity to the legible laws of an undoubted God.

Now there have as yet been three distinct schools of European architecture. I say, European, because Asiatic and African architectures belong so entirely to other races and climates, that there is no question of them here; only, in passing, I will simply assure you that whatever is good or great in Egypt, and Syria, and India, is just good or great for the same reasons as the buildings on our side of the Bosphorus. We Europeans, then, have had three great religions: the Greek, which was the worship of the God of Wisdom and Power; the Mediæval, which was the worship of the God of Judgment and Consolation; the Renaissance, which was the worship of the God of Pride and Beauty: these three we have had – they are past, – and now, at last, we English have got a fourth religion, and a God of our own, about which I want to ask you. But I must explain these three old ones first.

I repeat, first, the Greeks essentially worshipped the God of Wisdom; so that whatever contended against their religion, – to the Jews a stumbling-block, – was, to the Greeks – *Foolishness*.

The first Greek idea of deity was that expressed in the word, of which we keep the remnant in our words '*Di*-urnal' and '*Di*-vine' – the god of *Day*, Jupiter the revealer. Athena is his daughter, but especially daughter of the Intellect, springing armed from the head. We are only with the help of recent investigation beginning to penetrate the depth of meaning couched under the

Athenaic symbols: but I may note rapidly, that her ægis, the mantle with the serpent fringes, in which she often, in the best statues, is represented as folding up her left hand, for better guard; and the Gorgon, on her shield, are both representative mainly of the chilling horror and sadness (turning men to stone, as it were,) of the outmost and superficial spheres of knowledge – that knowledge which separates, in bitterness, hardness, and sorrow, the heart of the full-grown man from the heart of the child. For out of imperfect knowledge spring terror, dissension, danger, and disdain; but from perfect knowledge, given by the full-revealed Athena, strength and peace, in sign of which she is crowned with the olive spray, and bears the resistless spear.

This, then, was the Greek conception of purest Deity; and every habit of life, and every form of his art developed themselves from the seeking this bright, serene, resistless wisdom; and setting himself, as a man, to do things evermore rightly and strongly;[1] not with any ardent affection or ultimate hope; but with a resolute and continent energy of will, as knowing that for failure there was no consolation, and for sin there was no remission. And the Greek architecture rose unerring, bright, clearly defined, and self-contained.

Next followed in Europe the great Christian faith, which was essentially the religion of Comfort. Its great doctrine is the remission of sins; for which cause, it happens, too often, in certain phases of Christianity, that sin and sickness themselves are partly glorified, as if, the more you had to be healed of, the more divine was the healing. The practical result of this doctrine, in art, is a continual contemplation of sin and disease, and of imaginary states of purification from them; thus we have an architecture conceived in a mingled sentiment of melancholy and aspiration, partly severe, partly luxuriant, which will bend itself to every one of our needs, and every one of our fancies, and be strong or weak with us, as we are strong or weak ourselves. It is, of all architecture, the basest, when base people build it – of all, the noblest, when built by the noble.

And now note that both these religions – Greek and Mediæval – perished by falsehood in their own main purpose. The Greek religion of Wisdom perished in a false philosophy – 'Oppositions of science, falsely so called.' The Mediæval religion of Consolation perished in false comfort; in remission of sins given lyingly. It was the selling of absolution that ended the Mediæval faith; and I can tell you more, it is the selling of absolution which, to the end of time, will mark false Christianity. Pure Christianity gives her remission of sins only by *ending* them; but false Christianity gets her remission of sins by *compounding for* them. And there are many ways of compounding for them. We English have beautiful little quiet ways of buying absolution, whether in low Church or high, far more cunning than any of Tetzel's trading.

Then, thirdly, there followed the religion of Pleasure, in which all Europe gave itself to luxury, ending in death. First, *bals masqués* in every saloon, and then guillotines in every square. And all these three worships issue in vast temple building. Your Greek worshipped Wisdom, and built you the Parthenon – the Virgin's temple.

The Mediæval worshipped Consolation, and built you Virgin temples also – but to our Lady of Salvation. Then the Revivalist worshipped beauty, of a sort, and built you Versailles and the Vatican. Now, lastly, will you tell me what *we* worship, and what *we* build?

You know we are speaking always of the real, active, continual, national worship; that by which men act, while they live; not that which they talk of, when they die. Now, we have, indeed, a nominal religion, to which we pay tithes of property and sevenths of time; but we have also a practical and earnest religion, to which we devote nine-tenths of our property, and six-sevenths of our time. And we dispute a great deal about the nominal religion: but we are all unanimous about this practical one; of which I think you will admit that the ruling goddess may be best generally described as the 'Goddess of Getting-on,' or 'Britannia of the Market.' The Athenians had an 'Athena Agoraia,' or Athena of the Market; but she was a subordinate type of their goddess, while our Britannia Agoraia is the principal type of ours. And all your great architectural works are, of course, built to her. It is long since you built a great cathedral; and how you would laugh at me if I proposed building a cathedral on the top of one of these hills of yours, to make it an Acropolis! But your railroad mounds, vaster than the walls of Babylon; your railroad stations, vaster than the temple of Ephesus, and innumerable; your chimneys, how much more mighty and costly than cathedral spires! your harbour-piers; your warehouses; your exchanges! – all these are built to your great Goddess of 'Getting-on'; and she has formed, and will continue to form, your architecture, as long as you worship her; and it is quite vain to ask me to tell you how to build to *her*; you know far better than I.

There might, indeed, on some theories, be a conceivably good architecture for Exchanges – that is to say, if there were any heroism in the fact or deed of exchange, which might be typically carved on the outside of your building. For, you know, all beautiful architecture must be adorned with sculpture or painting; and for sculpture or painting, you must have a subject. And hitherto it has been a received opinion among the nations of the world that the only right subjects for either, were *heroisms* of some sort. Even on his pots and his flagons, the Greek put a Hercules slaying lions, or an Apollo slaying serpents, or Bacchus slaying melancholy giants, and earthborn despondencies. On his temples, the Greek put contests of great warriors in founding states, or of gods with evil spirits. On his houses and temples alike, the Christian put carvings of angels conquering devils; or of hero-martyrs exchanging this world for another: subject inappropriate, I think, to our direction of exchange here. And the Master of Christians not only left His followers without any orders as to the sculpture of affairs of exchange on the outside of buildings, but gave some strong evidence of His dislike of affairs of exchange within them. And yet there might surely be a heroism in such affairs; and all commerce become a kind of selling of doves, not impious. The wonder has always been great to me, that heroism has never been supposed to be in anywise consistent with the practice of supplying people with food, or clothes, but rather with that of quartering one's self upon them for food, and stripping them of their clothes. Spoiling of armour is an heroic deed in all ages; but the selling of clothes, old, or new, has never taken any colour of magnanimity. Yet one does not see why feeding the hungry and clothing the naked should ever become base businesses, even when engaged in on a large scale. If one could contrive to attach the notion of conquest to them anyhow! so that, supposing there were anywhere an obstinate race, who refused to be comforted, one might take some pride in giving them compulsory comfort!² and, as it were, '*occupying* a country' with one's gifts, instead of one's armies? If one could only consider it as much a victory to get a barren field sown, as to get an eared field stripped; and contend who should build villages, instead of who should 'carry' them! Are not all forms of heroism conceivable in doing these serviceable deeds? You doubt who is strongest? It might be ascertained by push of spade, as well as push of sword. Who is wisest? There are witty things to be thought of in planning other business than campaigns. Who is bravest? There are always the elements to fight with, stronger than men; and nearly as merciless.

The only absolutely and unapproachably heroic element in the soldier's work seems to be – that he is paid little for it – and regularly: while you traffickers, and exchangers, and others occupied in presumably benevolent business, like to be paid much for it – and by chance. I never can make out how it is that a *knight*-errant does not expect to be paid for his trouble, but a *pedlar*-errant always does; – that people are willing to take hard knocks for nothing, but never to sell ribands cheap; that they are ready to go on fervent crusades, to recover the tomb of a buried God, but never on any travels to fulfil the orders of a living one; – that they will go anywhere barefoot to preach their faith, but must be well bribed to practise it, and are perfectly ready to give the Gospel gratis, but never the loaves and fishes.[3]

If you chose to take the matter up on any such soldierly principle; to do your commerce, and your feeding of nations, for fixed salaries; and to be as particular about giving people the best food, and the best cloth, as soldiers are about giving them the best gunpowder, I could carve something for you on your exchange worth looking at. But I can only at present suggest decorating its frieze with pendant purses; and making its pillars broad at the base, for the sticking of bills. And in the innermost chambers of it there might be a statue of Britannia of the Market, who may have, perhaps advisably, a partridge for her crest, typical at once of her courage in fighting for noble ideas, and of her interest in game; and round its neck, the inscription in golden letters, 'Perdix fovit quæ non peperit.'[4] Then, for her spear, she might have a weaver's beam; and on her shield, instead of St George's Cross, the Milanese boar, semi-fleeced, with the town of Gennesaret proper, in the field; and the legend, 'In the best market,'[5] and her corslet, of leather, folded over her heart in the shape of a purse, with thirty slits in it, for a piece of money to go in at, on each day of the month. And I doubt not but that people would come to see your exchange, and its goddess, with applause.

Nevertheless, I want to point out to you certain strange characters in this goddess of yours. She differs from the great Greek and Mediæval deities essentially in two things – first, as to the continuance of her presumed power; secondly, as to the extent of it.

1st, as to the Continuance.

The Greek Goddess of Wisdom gave continual increase of wisdom, as the Christian Spirit of Comfort (or Comforter) continual increase of comfort. There was no question, with these, of any limit or cessation of function. But with your Agora Goddess, that is just the most important question. Getting on – but where to? Gathering together – but how much? Do you mean to gather always – never to spend? If so, I wish you joy of your goddess, for I am just as well off as you, without the trouble of worshipping her at all. But if you do not spend, somebody else will – somebody else must. And it is because of this (among many other such errors) that I have fearlessly declared your so-called science of Political Economy to be no science; because, namely, it has omitted the study of exactly the most important branch of the business – the study of *spending*. For spend you must, and as much as you make, ultimately. You gather corn: – will you bury England under a heap of grain; or will you, when you have gathered, finally eat? You gather gold: – will you make your house-roofs of it, or pave your streets with it? That is still one way of spending it. But if you keep it, that you may get more, I'll give you more; I'll give you all the gold you want – all you can imagine – if you can tell me what you'll do with it. You shall have thousands of gold pieces; – thousands of thousands – millions – mountains, of gold: where will you keep them? Will you put an Olympus of silver upon a golden Pelion – make Ossa like a wart? Do you think the rain and dew would then come down to you, in the streams from such mountains, more blessedly than they will down the mountains which God has made for you, of moss and whinstone? But it is not gold that you want to gather! What is it? greenbacks? No; not those neither. What is it then – is it ciphers after a capital I? Cannot you practise writing ciphers, and write as many as you want! Write ciphers for an hour every morning, in a big book, and say every evening, I am worth all those noughts more than I was yesterday. Won't that do? Well, what in the name of Plutus is it you want? Not gold, not greenbacks, not ciphers after a capital I? You will have to answer, after all, 'No; we want, somehow or other, money's *worth*.' Well, what is that? Let your Goddess of Getting-on discover it, and let her learn to stay therein.

II. But there is yet another question to be asked respecting this Goddess of Getting-on. The first was of the continuance of her power; the second is of its extent.

Pallas and the Madonna were supposed to be all the world's Pallas, and all the world's Madonna. They could teach all men, and they could comfort all men. But, look strictly into the nature of the power of your Goddess of Getting-on; and you will find she is the Goddess – not of everybody's getting on – but only of somebody's getting on. This is a vital, or rather deathful, distinction. Examine it in your own ideal of the state of national life which this Goddess is to evoke and maintain. I asked you what it was, when I was last here; – you have never told me. Now, shall I try to tell you?

Your ideal of human life then is, I think, that it should

be passed in a pleasant undulating world, with iron and coal everywhere underneath it. On each pleasant bank of this world is to be a beautiful mansion, with two wings; and stables, and coach-houses; a moderately-sized park; a large garden and hot-houses; and pleasant carriage drives through the shrubberies. In this mansion are to live the favoured votaries of the Goddess; the English gentleman, with his gracious wife, and his beautiful family; he always able to have the boudoir and the jewels for the wife, and the beautiful ball dresses for the daughters, and hunters for the sons, and a shooting in the Highlands for himself. At the bottom of the bank, is to be the mill; not less than a quarter of a mile long, with one steam engine at each end, and two in the middle, and a chimney three hundred feet high. In this mill are to be in constant employment from eight hundred to a thousand workers, who never drink, never strike, always go to church on Sunday, and always express themselves in respectful language.

Is not that, broadly, and in the main features, the kind of thing you propose to yourselves? It is very pretty indeed, seen from above; not at all so pretty, seen from below. For, observe, while to one family this deity is indeed the Goddess of Getting-on, to a thousand families she is the Goddess of *not* Getting-on. 'Nay,' you say, 'they have all their chance.' Yes, so has every one in a lottery, but there must always be the same number of blanks. 'Ah! but in a lottery it is not skill and intelligence which take the lead, but blind chance.' What then! do you think the old practice, that 'they should take who have the power, and they should keep who can,' is less iniquitous, when the power has become power of brains instead of fist? and that, though we may not take advantage of a child's or a woman's weakness, we may of a man's foolishness? 'Nay, but finally, work must be done, and some one must be at the top, some one at the bottom.' Granted, my friends. Work must always be, and captains of work must always be; and if you in the least remember the tone of any of my writings, you must know that they are thought unfit for this age, because they are always insisting on need of government, and speaking with scorn of liberty. But I beg you to observe that there is a wide difference between being captains or governors of work, and taking the profits of it. It does not follow, because you are general of an army, that you are to take all the treasure, or land, it wins; (if it fight for treasure or land;) neither, because you are king of a nation, that you are to consume all the profits of the nation's work. Real kings, on the contrary, are known invariably by their doing quite the reverse of this, – by their taking the least possible quantity of the nation's work for themselves. There is no test of real kinghood so infallible as that. Does the crowned creature live simply, bravely, unostentatiously? probably he *is* a King. Does he cover his body with jewels, and his table with delicates? in all probability he is *not* a King. It is possible he may be, as Solomon was; but that is when the nation shares his splendour with him. Solomon made gold, not only to be in his own palace as stones, but to be in Jerusalem as stones. But, even so, for the most part, these splendid kinghoods expire in ruin, and only the true kinghoods live, which are of royal labourers governing loyal labourers; who, both leading rough lives, establish the true dynasties. Conclusively you will find that because you are king of a nation, it does not follow that you are to gather for yourself all the wealth of that nation; neither, because you are king of a small part of the nation, and lord over the means of its maintenance – over field, or mill, or mine, – are you to take all the produce of that piece of the foundation of national existence for yourself.

You will tell me I need not preach against these things, for I cannot mend them. No, good friends, I cannot; but you can, and you will; or something else can and will. Even good things have no abiding power – and shall these evil things persist in victorious evil? All history shows, on the contrary, that to be the exact thing they never can do. Change *must* come; but it is ours to determine whether change of growth, or change of death. Shall the Parthenon be in ruins on its rock, and Bolton priory in its meadow, but these mills of yours be the consummation of the buildings of the earth, and their wheels be as the wheels of eternity? Think you that 'men may come, and men may go,' but – mills – go on for ever? Not so; out of these, better or worse shall come; and it is for you to choose which.

I know that none of this wrong is done with deliberate purpose. I know, on the contrary, that you wish your workmen well; that you do much for them, and that you desire to do more for them, if you saw your way to such benevolence safely. I know that even all this wrong and misery are brought about by a warped sense of duty, each of you striving to do his best; but, unhappily, not knowing for whom this best should be done. And all our hearts have been betrayed by the plausible impiety of the modern economist, telling us that, 'To do the best for ourselves, is finally to do the best for others.' Friends, our great Master said not so; and most absolutely we shall find this world is not made so. Indeed, to do the best for others, is finally to do the best for ourselves; but it will not do to have our eyes fixed on that issue. The Pagans had got beyond that. Hear what a Pagan says of this matter; hear what were, perhaps, the last written words of Plato, – if not the last actually written (for this we cannot know), yet assuredly in fact and power his parting words – in which, endeavouring to give full crowning and harmonious close to all his thoughts, and to speak the sum of them by the imagined sentence of the Great Spirit, his strength and his heart fail him, and the words cease, broken off for ever.

They are at the close of the dialogue called *Critias*, in which he describes, partly from real tradition, partly in ideal dream, the early state of Athens; and the genesis, and order, and religion, of the fabled isle of Atlantis; in which genesis he conceives the same first perfection and final degeneracy of man, which in our own Scriptural tradition is expressed by saying that the Sons of God inter-married with the daughters of men, for he supposes the earliest race to have been indeed the children of God; and to have corrupted themselves, until 'their spot was not the spot of his children.' And this, he says, was the end; that indeed 'through many generations, so long as the God's nature in them yet was full, they were sub-missive to the sacred laws, and carried themselves lovingly to all that had kindred with them in divineness; for their uttermost spirit was faithful and true, and in every wise great; so that, in *all meekness of wisdom, they dealt with each other*, and took all the chances of life; and despising all things except virtue, they cared little what happened day by day, and *bore lightly the burden* of gold and of possessions; for they saw that, if *only their common love and virtue increased, all these things would be increased together with them*; but to set their esteem and ardent pursuit upon material possession would be to lose that first, and their virtue and affection together with it. And by such reasoning, and what of the divine nature remained in them, they gained all this greatness of which we have already told; but when the God's part of them faded and became extinct, being mixed again and again, and effaced by the prevalent mortality; and the human nature at last exceeded, they then became unable to endure the courses of fortune; and fell into shapelessness of life, and baseness in the sight of him who could see, having lost everything that was fairest of their honour; while to the blind hearts which could not discern the true life, tending to happiness, it seemed that they were then chiefly noble and happy, being filled with all iniquity of inordinate possession and power. Whereupon, the God of Gods, whose Kinghood is in laws, beholding a once just nation thus cast into misery, and desiring to lay such punishment upon them as might make them repent into restraining, gathered together all the gods into his dwelling place, which from heaven's centre overlooks whatever has part in creation; and having assembled them, he said' –

The rest is silence. Last words of the chief wisdom of the heathen, spoken of this idol of riches; this idol of yours; this golden image, high by measureless cubits, set up where your green fields of England are furnace-burnt into the likeness of the plain of Dura: this idol, forbidden to us, first of all idols, by our own Master and faith; forbidden to us also by every human lip that has ever, in any age or people, been accounted of as able to speak according to the purposes of God. Continue to make that forbidden deity your principal one, and soon no more art, no more science, no more pleasure will be possible. Catastrophe will come; or, worse than catastrophe, slow mouldering and withering into Hades. But if you can fix some conception of a true human state of life to be striven for – life, good for all men, as for yourselves; if you can determine some honest and simple order of existence; following those trodden ways of wisdom, which are pleasantness, and seeking her quiet and withdrawn paths, which are peace;[6] – then, and so sanctifying wealth into 'commonwealth,' all your art, your literature, your daily labours, your domestic affection, and citizen's duty, will join and increase into one magnificent harmony. You will know then how to build, well enough; you will build with stone well, but with flesh better; temples not made with hands, but riveted of hearts; and that kind of marble, crimson-veined, is indeed eternal.

Notes

1. It is an error to suppose that the Greek worship, or seeking, was chiefly of Beauty. It was essentially of rightness and strength, founded on Forethought: the principal character of Greek art is not beauty, but design: and the Dorian Apollo-worship and Athenian Virgin-worship are both expressions of adoration of divine wisdom and purity. Next to these great deities, rank, in power over the national mind, Dionysus and Ceres, the givers of human strength and life; then, for heroic examples, Hercules. There is no Venus-worship among the Greeks in the great times: and the Muses are essentially teachers of Truth, and of its harmonies.

2. Quite serious, all this, though it reads like jest. [1873.]

3. Please think over this paragraph, too briefly and antithetically put, but one of those which I am happiest in having written. [1873.]

4. Jerem. xvii.11, (best in Septuagint and Vulgate). 'As the partridge, fostering what she brought not forth, so he that getteth riches, not by right, shall leave them in the midst of his days, and at his end shall be a fool.'

5. Meaning, fully, 'We have brought our pigs to it.' [1873.]

6. I imagine the Hebrew chant merely intends passionate repetition, and not a distinction of this somewhat fanciful kind; yet we may profitably make it in reading the English.

THE STORY OF PENGUIN CLASSICS

Before 1946 ... 'Classics' are mainly the domain of academics and students; readable editions for everyone else are almost unheard of. This all changes when a little-known classicist, E. V. Rieu, presents Penguin founder Allen Lane with the translation of Homer's *Odyssey* that he has been working on in his spare time.

1946 Penguin Classics debuts with *The Odyssey*, which promptly sells three million copies. Suddenly, classics are no longer for the privileged few.

1950s Rieu, now series editor, turns to professional writers for the best modern, readable translations, including Dorothy L. Sayers's *Inferno* and Robert Graves's unexpurgated *Twelve Caesars*.

1960s The Classics are given the distinctive black covers that have remained a constant throughout the life of the series. Rieu retires in 1964, hailing the Penguin Classics list as 'the greatest educative force of the twentieth century.'

1970s A new generation of translators swells the Penguin Classics ranks, introducing readers of English to classics of world literature from more than twenty languages. The list grows to encompass more history, philosophy, science, religion and politics.

1980s The Penguin American Library launches with titles such as *Uncle Tom's Cabin*, and joins forces with Penguin Classics to provide the most comprehensive library of world literature available from any paperback publisher.

1990s The launch of Penguin Audiobooks brings the classics to a listening audience for the first time, and in 1999 the worldwide launch of the Penguin Classics website extends their reach to the global online community.

The 21st Century Penguin Classics are completely redesigned for the first time in nearly twenty years. This world-famous series now consists of more than 1300 titles, making the widest range of the best books ever written available to millions – and constantly redefining what makes a 'classic'.

The Odyssey continues ...

The best books ever written

PENGUIN (P) CLASSICS

SINCE 1946

Find out more at www.penguinclassics.com